CITY OF GLASGOW (B) SQUADRON

602

602

AUXILIARY AIR FORCE

CAVE LEONEM CRUCIATUM

GLASGOW'S OWN

To those who founded the tradition, created the legend and followed after.

For I drift into the future, far as human eye could see,
Saw the Vision of the world, and all the wonder that would be;
Saw the heavens fill with commerce, argosies of magic sails,
Pilots of the purple twilight dropping down with costly bales;
Heard the heavens fill with shouting and there rained a ghostly dew
from the nations' airy navies grappling in the central blue.

Alfred Lord Tennyson
1830-1865

GLASGOW'S OWN

A VISUAL RECORD OF THE MEN AND MACHINES OF 602 (CITY OF GLASGOW) SQUADRON AUXILIARY AIR FORCE AND ROYAL AUXILIARY AIR FORCE 1925 to 1957

Dugald Cameron

No. 602 (City of Glasgow) Squadron,
was formed initially as a light day bomber squadron.
For a very short period in late 1938
it took-up army co-operation duties and
in January 1939 it became a fighter squadron,
a role in which it created an imperishable record
and a place of honour
in the annals and history of military flying.

Squadron Prints

GLASGOW

First published 1987 by
Squadron Prints Ltd.
3 Torrington Avenue, Giffnock, Glasgow G46 7LT

© 1987 Dugald Cameron

British Library Cataloguing in Publication Data
Cameron, Dugald
Glasgow's Own
1. Great Britain, *Royal Air Force*,
    Royal Auxiliary Air Force,
    Squadron 602—History
I. Title
358.4'14'0941   UG855.G7

ISBN 0-9512656-0-1

Designed by James W Murray

Typeset in Zapf Book Light by
Fraser Ross who also did the monochrome reproduction

Paper: Wiggins Teape Success Super Art and
High Speed Cartridge Grey

Colour origination by
Graphics + Four Ltd, Hull

Printed in Scotland by
Alna Press Ltd., Broxburn, West Lothian

The quality of many of the photographs
is poor. They are included for
their historical significance and in order
to present as complete a record
as possible.

CONTENTS

Nor law, nor duty bade me fight,
Nor public men, nor cheering crowds,
A lonely impulse of delight
Drove to this tumult in the clouds;

W B Yeats

AUTHOR'S PREFACE

In preparing and researching this material, I have had the great pleasure in meeting and talking to many of those whose service is celebrated within these pages, including most of the post-war Commanding Officers and Flight Commanders.

While it has not been too difficult to find many of the pilots, I have not been able to trace as many of the ground crew as I would have wished and none of the regular NCOs or airmen. Their story should be told, and their vital contribution properly recognised.

As many have said to me, this should have been done forty years ago. However I was but a school-boy then, my imagination fired by regular visits to Renfrew Airport to watch the Gods in their Vampires and Meteors, and dream of being there myself! My first aeronautical recollection was cycling over to Renfrew with my father on a summer Sunday morning during 1949 or 1950 and seeing the Spitfire 22's of 602. I recall noting these particular aircraft as being different from the pictures of the war time Spitfires in my books—how I wish I had persuaded my father to take the family Box-Brownie camera and capture them for posterity!

The impetus for this essay came from a meeting at Hillington with Bill McConnell (CO of No.2175 (Rolls Royce) Squadron ATC) and that 602 stalwart, Glen Niven, during September 1982. The formation of a 602 Museum Association to support the Museum which Bill McConnell and his team had under way was the necessary spur to realise my long held ambition to do something about it. It co-incided happily with the desire of my partner in Squadron Prints, Alan Carlaw and myself to select a subject with which to celebrate our one hundredth Squadron Print. Rolls-Royce generously agreed to sponsor the print with profits going to the 602 Museum. Having decided that it would be of a post-war 602 Spitfire, an enormous search was begun to seek-out photographic references for a Mark 22 and when this seemed unlikely to be successful it was decided to do a Mark 21, possibly the preserved one, LA198. At the time when the drawing had to be done, no photos of that aircraft in 602 service had come to light, thus its sister LA222 was chosen and became our subject.

Whilst carrying out this research, I became 'hooked' on 602 Squadron. It seemed a pity not to utilise properly the material which I had collected, hence the book. Its preparation has been a labour of love!

FOREWORD

by His Grace The Duke of Hamilton

In the last years of his life my father and I used to discuss the different aircraft we had flown and, sometimes wistfully, contemplate those we hadn't. Ironically, we both missed flying Spitfires operationally; he relinquished command of 602 Squadron two years before their introduction; I joined the last squadron in the Royal Air Force to fly them on active service two years after their withdrawal.

The Spitfire was only one of many aircraft operated by 602, but it is axiomatic that the Spitfire period of 1939-1951 was the Squadron's finest years just as the Battle of Britain was its finest hour.

The key factors in the Battle of Britain which made it possible to confront the German war machine on something like equal terms were the state of the art in airframe and engine development, fighter control and, not least, the proficiency and availability of aircrew. Camm & Mitchell, designers of the Hurricane and Spitfire, and Royce who masterminded the development programme which led from the 500 horsepower Eagle of the First World War to the over 2,000 horsepower Merlin of the Second, made enormous contributions to the effort, as did Watson Watt, the Father of Radar. None of their work, however, would have been to any avail had there been too few competent pilots. Even with the contribution of the auxiliaries, there was always a shortage, and pilot fatigue was one of the most serious problems of the battle.

The argument that high technology cannot be handled by part-timers is older than the Auxiliary Air Force. The fact that the first Syrian MIG destroyed over the Bekaa Valley was shot down by an Israeli reservist is ignored. The fact that American Air National Guard aircrew often reach higher standards of proficiency than their regular Navy or Airforce counterparts is ignored. The fact that one third of the pilots in the Battle of Britain were auxiliaries is ignored. It sometimes seems that Government and Civil Service minds unite in determination not to be "confused by the facts" but to continue the headlong rush towards more sophisticated and expensive equipment with fewer human beings to man it.

An example of this philosophy was the 'Sandys Axe' of 1957 which had a devastating effect on the British Aircraft Industry and grounded the Auxiliaries, yet led to only a trivial and temporary reduction in the defence budget. It is sobering to speculate on the outcome of the Battle of Britain had the axe fallen twenty years earlier; probably it would have been lost, with all the hideous consequences of Winston Churchill's "New Dark Age".

Dugald Cameron, Head of Design at the Glasgow School of Art, has researched this book with the same meticulous attention to detail for which he is renowned in his profiles and paintings. It will be of compelling interest to anyone concerned with the history or future of the volunteer element in the armed forces.

Lennoxlove,
East Lothian.
8th October 1987

INTRODUCTION

602, Glasgow's Flying Squadron
First in the Auxiliary Air Force
15th September 1925-10th March 1957.

The twentieth century has witnessed the remarkable and rapid development of aviation, from the tentative steps of the Wright brothers on the 17th December 1903, through the jet-age and into space.

The span of 602 Squadron's flying extends from that early classic trainer, the rotary-engined Avro 504K, along with the D.H.9A of First World War fame, to the RAF's first operational jets, the Meteor and Vampire. It also held the distinction of being the first Auxilary Air Force squadron to be equipped with the legendary Spitfire and, indeed, would seem to have flown that type of aircraft longer than any other squadron.

In the elegant pre-war days 602, like its fellow auxiliary squadrons, could be truly characterised as a "corps d'elite" with members coming from all walks of life. It consisted of artisans and executives from civilian life who were trained to the highest standards of proficiency required by the service and their efficiency, achieved by their dedication to the Squadron, was sufficient to allow them to take their place in the front-line at the outbreak of war. They faced the challenge with courage and rose triumphantly, making a notable contribution to the allied victory.

The Auxiliary Air Force was reformed in 1946 during the austere times and changed social and economic conditions of the subsequent peace. It later successfully made the transition to the jet-age.

The flying squadrons of the Royal Auxiliary Air Force were disbanded on 10th March 1957 but the vision of Trenchard, that a civilian, territorially based corps d'elite should be prepared to spend their spare-time flying in defence of their country, still remains valid. Even now, in the late 1980's, the Royal Auxiliary Air Force is increasing in size and significance albeit in the non-flying role. There is yet hope!

This account focuses upon 602 as an Auxiliary Squadron; however, its splendid and inspiring record during the War, could not be left out. Let it be a tribute to all who served with the Glasgow Squadron between 1925 and 1957 be they Auxiliary, Reserve or Regular.

A BRIEF HISTORY

As in so many other ways, the 'Father of the Royal Air Force', Marshal of the Royal Air Force Viscount Trenchard foresaw the need and value for a civilian manned auxiliary force organised and raised on a territorial basis. As early as in a 1919 memorandum, provision was made for an Air Force reserve. The antagonism of the Army and Navy to the fledgling Air Force as a whole and, no doubt, to arguments about the value of such forces, prevented the 1922 Bill, with its provision for Auxiliary and Special Reserve Squadrons, from becoming law until 1924. It was, however, enthusiastically promoted by the then Secretary of State for Air, Sir Samuel Hoare. Thus were the 'week-end' fliers eventually born!

Six Auxiliary and five Special Reserve Squadrons were proposed. The first to form was one of the latter, No.502 (County of Ulster) with the first true 'Auxiliary' Squadron being the subject of this book, No.602 (City of Glasgow), just ahead of No.601 (County of London). Officially the event dates from the arrival of the Adjutant, Flight Lieutenant Gilbert 'Dan' Martyn, to 602 Squadron on Saturday 12th September 1925 followed on the 14th by its first Commanding Officer, Squadron Leader C N Lowe MC DFC. He flew a DH9A (H144) from Henlow to Glasgow's Aerodrome at Renfrew on the 7th of October 1925—the very first flight by any aircraft of an Auxiliary Air Force Squadron.

The official date for 602's formation was Tuesday 15th September 1925, a date which was to have even greater significance fifteen years later! Also on the 15th September, the Squadron's permanent staff of thirteen NCOs and airmen arrived at Renfrew, the wartime 'acceptance aerodrome'. The first 'Auxiliaries' or 'week-end' airmen joined on 2nd November and over 200 applications were received that week. It was not intended that the Squadron should have a regular RAF CO, but Captain J D Latta MC, who had flown light scout aircraft during the 1914/18 war, was unable to take over command until February 1926 by which time he had undertaken the necessary conversion course on to the DH9A.

The Auxiliary Squadrons were unashamedly intended to be what they actually became, an 'élite'. A concept, applicable to both officers and men, which in present times is less happily accepted or understood. Then, however, in a quite different social climate, no doubts were entertained and in their early years up to World War II, the Auxiliary Squadrons were undoubtedly akin to the crack cavalry regiments in the skill which they displayed and the high morale which they engendered. The more stratified social divisions then apparent would now be unacceptable yet the high 'esprit de corps' and undoubted professional skill of the Auxiliary Air Force served this country magnificently in its hour of need during World War II. The contribution made by the Auxiliaries in the 'Battle of Britain' was second to none. It is significant that some Auxiliary Squadrons were re-equipped with Spitfires ahead of many regular units 602 Squadron being the first when Spitfire Is (K9961-K9979) were delivered to Abbotsinch from 8th May 1939. The concept of part-time civilian auxiliary forces is a fine one and in some countries (in particular the USA) they constitute vital components of their nation's total defence forces. The flying squadrons of the Royal Auxiliary Air Force were disbanded in March 1957, to be followed thereafter by the Light Anti-Aircraft Regiment Squadrons, and Fighter Control Units. However, the Royal Auxiliary Air Force and Royal Auxiliary Air Force Regiment still exist and include No.2 (City of Edinburgh) Maritime Headquarters Unit at RAF Pitreavie, Fife, together with airfield defence units such as 2622 (Highland) Squadron at RAF Lossiemouth, whose officers revived the wearing of the 'Grey Douglas' tartan kilt as their mess dress in 1983 (inaugurated by 602 in the 1930s).

Events in the life of 602 (City of Glasgow) Squadron

An élite—the pre-war squadron

1925	*12th September*	The Adjutant, Flt Lt G H 'Dan' Martyn, RAF, arrived at Renfrew—the 'Moorpark' aerodrome, signifying the formation of the Squadron.
	14th September	The first Commanding Officer arrived, Sqn Ldr C N Lowe, MC, DFC, RAF.
	15th September	602 (City of Glasgow) Squadron officially formed.
	7th October	DH9A (H144) flown from Henlow to Renfrew. Temporary town headquarters provided in the grounds of 52nd (Lowland Division) Signals Drill Hall in Jardine Street.
	2nd November	First auxiliary airmen enrolled.
1926	*1st February*	Capt J D Latta MC, took over as the Squadron's first Auxiliary CO.
	March	First parade of Squadron in uniform.
	April	Dr J C H Allen appointed medical officer. First Auxiliary pilots accepted, H G Davidson, J P Drew and C A S Parker.
	July	First annual camp at RAF Leuchars. All officers made parachute descents. Three DH9As and two Avro 504Ks available.
1927	*May*	Sqn Ldr Latta succeeded by Sqn Ldr J Fullerton as CO . Fullerton was later to sell his family mansion, Abbotsburn House on the River Cart, to the Air Ministry for use by the Squadron.
	12th July	New Town HQ at 49 Coplaw Street opened by H M King George V.
	July	Annual camp at RAF Leuchars.
	September	Fairey Fawns began to replace DH9As—more suitable for the cramped situation at Renfrew.
1928	*21st May*	First fatality on Squadron. Plt Off J P Drew killed in flying accident performing aerobatics in an Avro 504K.
1929	*31st July*	First Westland Wapiti delivered from Yeovil by Flt Lt, The Marquess of Douglas and Clydesdale.
	July	Annual camp at RAF Leuchars with six Fawns and four Avro 504Ns.
	22nd November	Esher Trophy (for the top Auxiliary Squadron) presented to 602 at the City Chambers, Glasgow by Marshal of the Royal Air Force, Viscount Trenchard.
1930	*7th June*	Flying display at Renfrew organised by the Squadron.
	July	Annual camp. RAF Leuchars.
	29th July	Wapitis J9602 and J9094, collided when taking off at RAF Leuchars—no casualties.
	1st August	Urgent medical supplies flown to Islay in Avro 504N J9705 by Lloyd and Powell. This was possibly the first aircraft to land on the island and was the precursor of the Scottish Air Ambulance Service. Lloyd later said, "A fellow came to the

mess in rather a state because there was a woman who was dying of tetanus on the island of Islay. The Scottish Flying Club was closed—I could not think of a better excuse for pinching an Avro—by boat the medicine would take over 24 hours to reach her."

	October	The Squadron was runner-up in RAF's Laurence Minot Bombing Competition. Pilot Douglas Farquhar; gunner/bomb-aimer R B Clark.
1931	*7th March*	Aerial collision between Avro 504N and Wapiti, pilots Phillips and Land killed, gunner Smith parachuted to safety.
	May	Rev Lewis Sutherland appointed Padre—he did not retire until 1952!
	July	Annual camp RAF Hawkinge.
1932	*May*	Sqn Ldr, the Marquess of Douglas and Clydesdale (later 14th Duke of Hamilton and Brandon) appointed CO.
	July	Annual camp RAF Hawkinge. During 1932, Flt Lt D F MacIntyre was seconded to No.12 (Bomber) Squadron RAF to gain operational experience.
1933	*20th January*	The Squadron moved to its new base at RAF Abbotsinch near Paisley replacing the leased quarters at Renfrew. Among the first service aircraft to land was a Squadron Wapiti flown by D F MacIntyre and G C Pinkerton. (It is ironic that MacIntyre was to subsequently plan and develop Prestwick airport.)
	3rd April	The CO, The Marquess of Douglas and Clydesdale, together with its next CO Flt Lt D F MacIntyre, became the first men to fly over Mount Everest—both were awarded the Air Force Cross.
	June	HM King George V approved the wearing of the kilt by the pipe bands of the two Scottish Auxiliary Squadrons, 602 and 603 (City of Edinburgh). Appropriately the tartan chosen was the Duke of Hamilton's Grey Douglas. (Colours, black, white and grey).
	July	Annual camp at RAF Hawkinge.
1934	*July*	Annual camp at RAF Lympne.
1935	*February*	Wapitis replaced by Hawker Harts.
	July	Annual camp at RAF North Coates Fittes, 602 being the first Auxiliary Squadron to participate in an Armament Practice there. They are reported to have fired 13,600 rounds of ammunition and dropped 529 bombs with great success. Royal Review at RAF Mildenhall, the Squadron being represented by Farquhar, Rintoul and Selway.
	9th August	*Historical note:*—Scottish Aviation Ltd incorporated at Prestwick. Formed by 602's Clydesdale and MacIntyre. Prestwick today still supports a significant Scottish aircraft industry and international 'gateway' airport.
1936	*February*	*Historical note:*—Prestwick opened as a grass flying field by D F MacIntyre.
	April	Fighter affiliation exercises with the Bristol Bulldogs of 17 (Fighter) Squadron.
	June	Hawker Hinds replaced the Harts.
	July	Annual camp at RAF Tangmere.
	July	Approval given for the 'Grey Douglas' tartan kilt to be worn with Mess Dress by Auxiliary Officers of 602 and 603.
	September	Sqn Ldr David MacIntyre assumed command.

1937		New Squadron badge in standard RAF format approved by HM King George VI.
	July	Annual camp at Rochford (Southend Airport).
	October	Sqn Ldr A D Farquhar appointed to command.
1938	*3rd May*	In company with Nos. 269 and 603 Squadrons, 602 provided a flypast for the opening of the great Glasgow Empire Exhibition by the King.
	July	Annual camp at RAF Hawkinge.
	29th October	Three Hinds flown by Pinkerton, MacKellar and Webb collaborated with searchlights to mark the closing of the Empire Exhibition in what was then a record for night-flying among Auxiliary Squadrons.
	1st November	Squadron transferred from 2 (Bomber) Group to 22 (Army Co-operation) Group, and with it a change of role. Hawker Hectors replaced the Hinds.
1939	*14th January*	602 became a fighter squadron and transferred to 13 (Fighter) Group. Gloster Gauntlet fighter aircraft replaced the Hectors.
	March	Two Fairey Battle aircraft delivered to introduce pilots to modern monoplanes with retractable undercarriage—anticipating 602's future equipment
	April	LAC Phillips volunteered to be first NCO pilot in the Auxiliary Air Force.
	8th May	Spitfires delivered! 602 was the first Auxiliary Squadron to be equipped with the RAF's new fighter and among the first in the Air Force as a whole—an acknowledgement of its prowess. The Squadron operated various Marks of Spitfires throughout the War.
		When the Spitfires arrived, they were immediately locked away in the hangars to the dismay of all, or all except 602's then adjutant. There were procedures to be followed, red-tape to be untangled. Having been egged-on by Archie McKellar, a constant critic of bureaucracy, George Pinkerton OC 'B' Flight, took matters into his own hands and, under the pretext of checking the guns, finally got one out of the hangar and into the air. The 'boys' soon followed suit!
	July	Annual camp at RAF Church Fenton.
	24th August	Call-up! 602 Squadron embodied into the Royal Air Force in anticipation of the outbreak of war. Squadron strength—22 officers and 174 airmen commanded by Sqn Ldr Douglas Farquhar at RAF Abbotsinch.

A number of the pre-war pilots had learned to fly with the Scottish Flying Club which began operations at Renfrew in 1926 the year after the Squadron's inauguration. A number of flying competitions were held between the two organisations including the Fullerton Trophy presented by John Fullerton a former CO of 602. George Pinkerton, Vivian Bell, Finlay Boyd and Dunlop Urie all took their 'A' licence with the SFC before being commissioned into 602 and Pinkerton was the last Chairman of the SFC in the mid 1950s. David McIntyre and Douglas Farquhar got their licences with the shorter lived Beardmore Flying School, the SFC was charging 30 shillings solo and 40 shillings dual throughout the thirties. The cost of the 'A' Licence was refunded by the Air Ministry on commissioning up to a maximum of £115.

The pre-war period created an élite. The social life being almost as important as the flying—yet the time was soon to come when their operational efficiency was to be tested. They did not fail.

The Challenge of War

1939		
	3rd September	Britain declared war on Germany.
	8 September	Sgt Bryden killed on first night flight in Spitfire I, K9965.
	7th October	One Flight of 602 moved to RAF Grangemouth on a daily basis.
	13th October	Squadron transfered to RAF Drem near North Berwick to provide escorts for east-coast convoys and defend naval installations in the Firth of Forth.
	16th October	In the morning, 'B' Flight led by Flt Lt George Pinkerton, was scrambled to intercept an enemy raid. Pinkerton fired at one aircraft which was seen to disappear, smoking, into cloud, but the result was inconclusive. In the afternoon 602 were again in action along with 603. Both Squadrons intercepted an enemy raid on shipping in the Forth. Pinkerton and McKellar downed a Ju88 of KG30 off Crail and Gifford of 603 (what was reported as) an He111 which crashed at Port Seton.
		An argument as to whether 602 or 603 were first to draw blood has since continued, but what can be said is that to both Auxiliary Squadrons goes the honour of participation in the first Fighter Command actions of World War II. In fact four enemy aircraft were shot down that day by the Glasgow and Edinburgh Squadrons.
	28th October	602 and 603 Squadrons again saw action and shared in the shooting down of a Heinkel 111 of KG26 which came down substantially intact at Humbie—the first enemy aircraft to be brought down on British soil since World War I and Archie McKellar's first victory—the first of many.
	24th November	George Pinkerton posted to command the Regular, No.65 Squadron—the first Auxiliary to fill such a post. Flt Lt Sandy Johnstone now OC 'B' Flight.
	26th November	George Pinkerton awarded the DFC for his efforts on the 16th October. This, with that of Pat Gifford of 603, were the first to be awarded in Fighter Command and the second in the Royal Air Force as a whole.
	21st December	Most regrettably, a section of 602 shot down two RAF Hampden aircraft of 44 Squadron which were returning from a raid, one Hampden crew member being killed. The subsequent Court of Inquiry cleared the fighter squadron of blame.
1940	*22nd February*	Sqn Ldr Farquhar shot down a Heinkel 111 which force landed near Coldingham. Farquhar landed beside it to prevent its destruction, but, due to wet ground, overturned and had to be released by the enemy airmen!
	26th February	HM King George VI visited RAF Drem, along with Air Marshal Dowding, AOC in C Fighter Command and decorated Farquhar with a DFC.
	April	Sqn Ldr George Pinkerton DFC returned to take command from Douglas Farquhar on the latter's promotion to command RAF Martlesham Heath.
	25th April	Flt Lt Marcus Robinson promoted to command 616 (South Yorkshire) Squadron. Flt Lt J D Urie now OC 'A' Flight.

14th April	'A' Flight moved to RAF Montrose and 'B' Flight to RAF Dyce.
28th May	Squadron returned to RAF Drem.
May	Flt Lt Archie McKellar left to become a flight commander on 605 Squadron.
July	Sqn Ldr Sandy Johnstone took command.

During their stay at Drem, 602 had well and truly opened their account with the enemy, 13 Group achieved their 50th kill on the 9th of July when Donald Jack and Dunlop Urie attacked a pair of Ju88s. Urie downed one and Jack severly damaged the other. Pinkerton had opened the batting followed by Farquhar, McKellar, MacLean, Strong, Robinson, Johnstone, Webb, Boyd, Urie, Jack and McDowall. Pinkerton and Farquhar had been decorated with DFCs. The pre-war stalwarts had proved their worth.

12th August	602 is ordered to move south to RAF Westhampnett, RAF Tangmere's satellite on the south coast near Chichester, within 11 (Fighter) Group—in the front-line of the Battle of Britain.
13th August	Arrived at Westhampnett.
14th August	In Action!
15th August	Dornier shot down.
16th August	Tangmere attacked by Ju87's.
18th August	Dunlop Urie took off in newly delivered Spitfire X4110, and crash landed it twenty minutes later after combat. Aircraft damaged beyond repair—possibly the shortest operational life of any aircraft. Dunlop Urie to hospital.
15th September	Fighter Command's greatest day and the virtual end to the invasion threat—since designated 'Battle of Britain Day'.

Signal from HQ 11 Group, 29th October 1940—"Group Commander sends warmest congratulations to 602 Squadron on their magnificent combat at mid-day when they destroyed eight fighters and shot-down two others without loss of pilots or aircraft creating a record for months past."

602's success can be traced to the effective leadership and inspiration which David McIntyre instilled during his period as Commanding Officer; he was a superb airman and the experience he gained with 12 Squadron led him to institute a proper training syllabus which "converted 602 from being a kind of flying club into a truly professional Squadron and, by the outbreak of war they also had an unusually high level of night flying experience". Sadly David McIntyre was killed in December 1957 on an overseas sales mission in one of his own Scottish Aviation Twin Pioneers. Thus began 602 Squadron's contribution to the winning of what became known as the 'Battle of Britain' and for Glasgow's 'Few' an assured place in the role of honour. These men, lead by Sqn Ldr Sandy Johnstone were, Ellis Aries, Cyril Babbage, Paddy Barthropp, Finlay Boyd, Sgt Bracton, 'Roger' Coverley, Alfred Eade, Jake Edy, 'Ian' Ferguson, Douglas Gage, 'Pedro' Hanbury, J S Hart, John Willy Hopkin, Donald Jack, 'Pat' Lyall, Hector McLean, Andrew McDowall, Harry Moody, 'Micky' Mount, Glen Niven, 'Agony' Payne, Randall Philips, J Proctor, Glyn Ritchie, Nigel Rose, W B Smith, M H Sprague, Dunlop Urie, Paul Webb, 'Ginger' Whall and 'Wimpy' Whipps.

Sadly, Moody, Coverley, Sprague and Whall were lost during the Battle and Edy, Gage, Hanbury, Lyall, Ritchie and Whipps were to be killed in action later in the war.

This inspiring achievement was made possible only by the courage of the pilots and the dedication and skill of those on the ground, from the youngest aircraftsman to the Commanding Officer.

17th December	Squadron ordered to Prestwick for rest and recuperation. Aircraft exchanged with those of 610 Squadron at RAF Acklington on the way north.

1941

March	602 main flying participants in the film 'A Yank in the RAF', made at Prestwick.
13th March	Clydeside Blitz—'Fighter Night' tactics in operation with 602 defending their own City—ironically, due to organisational difficulties, not too successful.
15th April	Moved from RAF Prestwick to the new satellite airfield at Heathfield, RAF Ayr.
April	Sqn Ldr J I Kilmartin now in command.
May	Glasgow and Clydeside attacked. 602 in action.
June	Sqn Ldr P E Meagher took command with Flt Lt Al Deere as a flight commander.
10th June	Rudolf Hess parachuted from a Me110 into Eaglesham near Glasgow to seek out fellow flier the Duke of Hamilton (formerly Marquess of Douglas and Clydesdale).
	By now few of the original Auxiliaries remained with the Squadron.
July	To RAF Kenley for strike operations over the Channel. Took part in 'Circuses' with 200 or more fighters; 'Rodeos', large scale fighter sweeps; 'Ramrods', bomber escort duties; 'Roadsteads', attacks on coastal shipping and 'Rhubarbs', low-level sorties by a few fighters.
August	Sqn Ldr Al Deere assumed command.
1st November	Sqn Ldr Archibald Ashmore McKellar, DSO, DFC and Bar, Auxiliary Air Force, officer commanding 605 Squadron, and previously with 602, killed in action. One of Glasgow's immortal 'Few'.

1942

January	Sqn Ldr Paddy Finucane appointed CO.
14th January	Moved to Redhill.
12th February	Wg Cdr Finlay Boyd (ex-602) in company with Gp Capt Victor Beamish, sighted the German battlecruisers Scharnhorst and Gneisenau during their dash up the Channel; unfortunately later efforts to deal with the ships were unsuccessful.
4th March	Moved back to RAF Kenley.
June	Sqn Ldr P M Brothers assumed command.
17th July	Moved to RAF Peterhead.
19th August	Under Sqn Ldr Pete Brothers, the Squadron successfully played its part in providing fighter cover during the Dieppe Raid, shooting down five enemy aircraft and damaging nine others.
	Those successful included Flt Lt Eric Bocock, Fg Off Rippon, Plt Off Ralph Sampson, and Sergeants Caldercote, Hauser, Lothbridge, Loud and Marryshaw.
	Plt Off M F Goodchap was shot down to become a Prisoner of War and Flt Lt Johnny Niven was rescued by the Royal Navy having been downed in the Channel. He recovered in Brighton Hospital.
10th September	'A' Flight moved to RAF Skeabrae in Orkney and 'B' Flight to Sumburgh, on Shetland. Spitfire VIs were used for high level interceptions of German aircraft on reconnaissance missions over Scapa Flow.

	October	Sqn Ldr M F Beytagh now in command.
1943	*20th January*	To RAF Perranporth for shipping escort duties.
	14th April	To RAF Lasham.
	29th April	To RAF Fairlop.
	1st June	To RAF Bognor.
	1st July	To RAF Kingsnorth.
	13th August	To RAF Newchurch.
	28th September	Sgt Pierre Clostermann (Free French Air Force and author of 'The Big Show') posted to 602. One of the many allied airmen to serve with the Squadron.
	12th October	To RAF Detling, the Squadron now equipped with Spitfire IXs.
	October	Squadron now commanded by Sqn Ldr Max Sutherland.
	15th November	Squadron transferred to 2nd Tactical Air Force, 83 Group, 125 Wing. Offensive sweeps over France and escort duties.
1944	*18th January*	Moved back to RAF Skeabrae under 12 Group with Spitfire Vs ('clipped, clapped and cropped')! Due to fog, the Squadron went by rail, then boat. Included in their complement of aircraft were a few Spitfire VIIs, 'Strato Spits' for high altitude interceptions.
	20th February	At Skeabrae in the Orkneys. Plt Off Ian Blair DFM in Strato-Spit, MD114 shot down a high-flying Bf109G Recce aircraft—something of a record.
	13th March	To RAF Llanbedr with Spitfire IXs. 602 and 132 Squadrons were to be guinea pigs in experiments to fit Spitfires with 500lb bombs for attacks on the German V1 flying-bomb sites.
	20th March	To RAF Detling.
	18th April	To RAF Ford in preparation for 'D' Day.
	6th June	'D' Day, invasion of Europe. 602 provided low cover for the landing craft.
	25th June	Squadron began operating from Normandy, initially at Airfield B11 (Longues). Therafter the Squadron performed in the ground attack and strafing role flying from a number of airfields in Northern Europe.
	7th July	Sqn Ldr Chris Le Roux took command. He was killed in action soon after in a flying accident.
	August	Sqn Ldr Max Sutherland returned as CO.
	13th August	At B19 (Lingevres Airfield).
	2nd September	At B40 (Nivilliers Airfield).
	17th September	At B70 (Deurne Airfield).
	29th September	Squadron returned to the UK and was based at RAF Coltishall.
	18th October	To RAF Matlaske, and re-equipped with Spitfire L.F. XVIs, for attacks on the V2 rocket launching sites.
	1st December	Attacked the V2 sites on the first 'Big Ben' mission—this one beside the Royal Palace in The Hague.
1945	*23rd February*	To RAF Ludham, continued offensive strike operations over Holland and into Germany.

18th March	Attacked the Shell Mex building in the Hague housing a variety of German scientists and workers—a remarkable low-level raid planned and led by Max Sutherland with Raymond Baxter on his wing.
8th May	'VE' Day, end of the European War.
15th May	602 (City of Glasgow) Squadron disbanded and was credited with destruction of 150 enemy aircraft. The challenge of war was fully met.

This brief selection of events does scant justice to the heroism, skill and dedication of the men of 602, and gives only a hint of their part in securing victory for the allied cause. Many were the Honours won and decorations awarded and, sadly, lives laid down.

602 had a 'good war'. From their early encounters with the enemy in Scottish skies and their success in the 'Battle of Britain', under the leadership of Sandy Johnstone, they participated in fighter sweeps across the Channel, the Dieppe Raid and defended Scapa Flow before preparing for the invasion of Europe. They later gave support across the Channel in Normandy and Northern Europe and finally attacked targets in the Low Countries paying particular attention to the V1 and V2 rocket sites.

They had been commanded by some of the RAF's most distinguished fighter pilots; Farquhar, Pinkerton and Johnstone of the pre-war auxiliary band who were followed by Deere, Finucane, Brothers, Beytagh, Sutherland and le Roux. Others who had served with them like Boyd, Jack, MacLean, McDowall, McKellar, Mount, Robinson, Urie, and Webb made their own contribution to the legend and went on to command other squadrons.

Many were those who fought with 602 and whose names find an honoured place in its history. Glen 'Nuts' Niven who defied authority to fly with only 602 and his namesake Johnny Niven, Bill Loud, 'Ginger' Lacey—one of the RAF's top scorers who shot-down the Heinkel which had attacked Buckingham Palace—and Tommy Williams from 611 Squadron, another Auxiliary. Eric Bocock, Joe Kistruck, Strudwick and Freeborn all played their part. Ian Blair who had won the DFM on Blenheims and George Hannah were among the few Glaswegians to fly with 602 during the later stages of the war. Then there were the Canadians, Bob Gourlay and 'Moose' Manson; McKenzie and Morgan from New Zealand; Finnie and Dumbrell from Australia; Aubertin and the terrible twins Remlinger and Clostermann from the Free French, the latter telling his own story in the 'Big Show'. Others like Tommy Maggs, Jimmy Kelly, Frank Wooley, 'Mac' McConachie, Ken Charney and Roy Hook were also involved and latterly , Dickie Pertwee, 'Fearless' Pullman, Cec Zuber, 'Steve' Stephenson and Raymond Baxter—the latter to become a 'weel kent' voice and face with the BBC and Tommy 'Cupid' Love possibly the last Glasgwegian to fly operationally with 602 and certainly one of the RAF's smallest pilots! All were supported by the commitment and skill of that un-sung band of heroes, the ground crews. It had originally been intended that they would remain with the Squadron throughout the war but few remained by 1945, one being Sgt Alfie MacDonald, a fitter, who had first joined the Squadron in 1929. The legend was created by them too.

Many of that pre-war 602 'élite' survived the conflict ending up in senior ranks. Marcus Robinson, Finlay Boyd and George Pinkerton retired as Group Captains with Donald Jack, Dunlop Urie and Andy McDowall as Wing Commanders. McDowall, who joined 602 from the RAFVR in 1939 as a Sergeant Pilot, commanded 616 Squadron, the RAF's first Meteor jet-fighter unit and after the war became a test pilot with Rolls-Royce. Edward Howell, who had transferred to the regular RAF before the war was leading fighter squadrons during the fall of Crete in the spring of 1941. His escape and return to his country, despite severe injury, is the inspiring subject of his book 'Escape to Live'.

Problems of Peace

Soon after the end of the War, the government announced that the Auxiliary Air Force was to be reformed.

1946	11th June	(From 602's Operations Record Book). "As a result of a decision by the Air Ministry, to reform; auxiliary Squadrons, 602 City of Glasgow, Auxiliary Air Force was reformed with quarters on RNAS Abbotsinch under the command of Sqn Ldr M Robinson AFC." Flt Lt D O Cunliffe DFC arrived to take up the position of Adjutant. 602 Squadron were once more in business as a Fighter Squadron.
	6th August	Assistant Adjutant, Flt Lt M W Grierson-Jackson arrived.
	14th August	First aircraft, Harvard T2B, KF374, delivered from 10MU Hullavington.
	24th August	Harvard T2B, KF584, collected by Flt Lt Jackson from 7 SFTS Kirton-in-Lindsey.
	1st September	Sqn Ldr Marcus Robinson AFC gazetted as Commanding Officer, 602 Squadron, Auxiliary Air Force.
	30th September	Re-decoration of Town HQ at Coplaw Street completed. Flying hours for September, 10.35.
	1st October	Weekend working commenced. Regular personnel were granted leave on Tuesday and Wednesday in lieu of Saturday/Sunday—circumstances permitting!
	22nd October	Spitfire FR14E, TP236, allotted to 602 Squadron—first post-war operational aircraft. Reserve Command indentification letters 'RAI' together with the individual aircraft letter began to appear.
	8th November	Recruiting started at Town HQ. Fg Off G Hume arrived as regular Engineering Officer.
	20th November	Recruiting in progress—150 applications.
	1st December	The second Spitfire FR14E arrived, TX985.
	31st December	Squadron strength—3 Officers
		34 Airmen
		1 Auxiliary Commanding officer
		Flying hours for December, 6.3
		Harvard, 2.75, Spitfire 3.55

1947	22nd January	First Sergeant pilots attested and inducted into the Auxiliary Air Force as NCO airmen.
	2nd February	Flying by NCO pilots began with dual instruction on the Harvard.
	March	Commissions in hand for A W (Archie) Robinson and Alex Richardson.
	April	Flt Lt A R Stewart inducted as Senior Medical Officer. He served the Squadron throughout the entire post-war period but was later killed in the Trident crash at Staines in 1972.
		Evening training commenced on Mondays and Thursdays.
	22nd June	Fg Off Archie Robinson DFC made a forced-landing at Abbotsinch in Spitfire F14, RM753, due to an engine fault—pilot unhurt, aircraft written-off.
	19th July	Annual camp (first since war) at RAF Woodvale. Seven Spitfires and two Harvards arrived by air, ground party by train. Returned on 2nd August.
	31st July	Fg Off Ivor Reid killed in flying accident, near Fleetwood in Spitifre F21, LA211. Flying hours for July 172.45.
	August	The Squadron was stood-down for the month. This was later to become the norm.
	6th September	Flying restarted.
	27th September	Glasgow holiday weekend, evening flying finished for year.
	1st October	AOC's inspection by Air Commodore Burns.
	November	Evening training at Coplaw Street with lectures on meteorology, accident prevention and navigation.
	16th December	'Royal' title granted to the Auxiliary Air Force by H M King George VI.
	22nd December	Recruiting slow in the ground trades but was expected to pick-up after a show in the Kelvin Hall during February.
1948	20th February	Visit by Air Marshal, Lord Tedder, to open Territorial Show in Kelvin Hall.
	February	"Flying restricted due to only 3 Spitfires, on average, being serviceable at weekend."
	3rd April	Fg Off Hamish McWilliam killed in flying accident near Bishopton in Spitfire F21, LA268.
	2nd May	Interception of "Harvard bomber force" by two sections of Spitfires.
	3rd May	Night flying commenced in Harvards.
	9th May	3 Spitfires carried out successful interceptions with 1830 Squadron RNVR (also based at RNAS Abbotsinch).
	23rd May	Interception exercise with 3 Mosquitos of 502 Squadron, RAF Aldergrove, Northern Ireland.
	16th July	7 Spitfires led by CO left Abbotsinch for annual camp at RAF Tangmere.
	31st October	P2. Jim Johnston, who had flown Mosquitos in the Far East and won the DFC, force-landed a Spitfire F21 near Glenboig due to engine-failure—LA222 a write-off, pilot unhurt.
	1st November	Abbotsburn House (pre-war officers' mess of 602) handed back to Squadron. Top three rooms furnished as married quarters for Adjutant and Assistant Adjutant.

	21st December	Auxiliary Strength—8 Auxiliary Officers
		7 NCO pilots
		74 Auxiliary Airmen
	Aircraft	3 Harvard T2Bs
		12 Spitfire F21 and F22s.

1949   *6/12/13th March*   602 Squadron participated in large scale Forth/Clyde exercise—38 sorties being completed.

31st March   "March better than February, from flying viewpoint". Weather, particularly fog, had always been a problem to flying in the West of Scotland.

23rd June   After incidents due to the poor state of 'runways' at Abbotsinch, all Spitfire flying was cancelled.

27th June   At a conference it was decided that the Squadron would operate from Renfrew airport meanwhile, thus 602 returned to its birthplace of 1925. Official sanction was sought for the permanent use of Renfrew.

July   Annual camp at RAF Horsham St Faith during which 6 Spitfires attended the fortieth anniversary of Blériot's channel crossing at Le Touquet. After much hospitality, Fg Off Forrest was prevailed upon to demonstrate the Spitfire. He describes his performance in his log-book as "demonstration tres dangereux"!

17th September   Battle of Britain Day. Fg Off Melling won the high speed race at RAF Dyce.

1st November   602 was transferred to Fighter Command, and the Squadron's old identification letters 'LO' were able to be used again (although they weren't actually painted on until mid 1950).

"602 based at Abbotsinch where all major servicing and administrative work is carried out. All flying however takes place from Renfrew aerodrome some 6 miles away by road."

Aircraft serviceability presents problems. By 20th of month "all Spitfires still unserviceable".

"Recruiting auxiliary personnel poor—improved transport arrangements to be provided to and from Glasgow WEF on last week in December."

31st December   Auxiliary strength of 10 pilots, 6 ground officers, 85 airmen.
Flying for December—

	Day	Night
Harvard	13 sorties (12.10 hrs)	2 sorties (1.30 hrs)
Spitfire 21	24 sorties (20.15 hrs)	
Spitfire 22	3 sorties (1.45 hrs)	

1950   *24th February*   Re-union Dinner at Town HQ for past and present members to commemorate 25th Anniversary of 602's formation. Sqn Ldr Marcus Robinson commented on 602's low position on Fighter Command's jet priority list—'particularly disappointing in view of Renfrew's availability for jet aircraft operation'.

13th March   Combined recruiting exercise at 12 Argyle Street, Glasgow by 602, 2602 (Royal Auxiliary Air Force Regiment Squadron) and 3602 (Fighter Control Unit)—by 25th March 37 names!

	14th July	During evening, 10 Spitfires and 3 Harvards took-off from Renfrew for annual camp at RAF Chivenor.
	September	Marcus Robinson, having completed his statutory five years in command, handed over to Sqn Ldr H M Stephen DSO DFC.
	3rd November	Informal discussion from flying control viewpoint on subject of jet operation from Renfrew.
	2nd December	Flt Lt A A V Maxwell, Training Officer to 226 OCU at RAF Stradishall for a short conversion course on Vampire 5 aircraft. "602 to be re-equipped with Vampire 5 at earliest opportunity and all necessary administrative arrangements are in hand".
	9th December	"All efforts are being made to reduce Spitfire holding on 602 to 6 aircraft to enable delivery of jets to be effected." During 1950, 602 flew 1384 hours, an increase of approximately 36% on 1949.
1951	7th January	"Only two Spitfire sorties flown due to poor weather."
	13th January	At last the jet-age came to Clydeside with the delivery of two de-Havilland Vampire FB5 aircraft to Renfrew—VZ831 and WA232. Two pilots carried out their first solos on them—other flying limited due to poor serviceability of Spitfires.
	27th January	Press visited 602 at Renfrew and were given trips in two Meteor T7s borrowed for the occasion; VZ633, ZD-Z (222 Squadron) and WA729 both from RAF Leuchars.
	30th January	Re-equipping with Vampires almost completed, eight aircraft having been delivered during January. Most pilots made their first solos on the new jet aircraft thereafter.
	15th April	602 Squadron mobilised! With the outbreak of the Korean War in the previous June and the increasingly hostile situation it was decided to mobilize all the Auxiliary fighter squadrons for three months continuous training. 602 were to spend their time at RAF Leuchars.
	26th April	7 Vampires, 1 Meteor T7 and 1 Harvard flew to RAF Acklington for Armament Practice Camp.
	8th May	Fg Off MacGregor ferried "last" Spitfire PK651, LO-N to RAF North Luffenham (there were actually three left behind at Renfrew), twelve years to the day after the first were delivered to 602 in 1939. This gave 602 the longest record of any RAF Squadron with this type of aircraft.
	23rd June	Caught by an East Coast haar, Fg Off Anderson of 603 Squadron was killed force-landing one of 602's Meteor T7s (VW438).
	29the June	With 43 and 222, the resident Leuchar's Squadrons, 602 participated in Exercise "Silver Strand" operating from Prestwick.
	13th July	Having completed their 'call-up', 602 returned to Renfrew receiving congratulations from AOC-in-C Fighter Command on the progress made.
	25th August	Flt Sgt Harry Henderson received the BEM from Air Marshal Sir Basil Embry at a parade at Leuchars.
1952	April	One of 602's Meteor T7s modified for target-towing. 602 were believed to be the first Auxiliary Squadron in No. 12F Group to carry out Air-to-Air (Flag) Gunnery.

	July	Annual camp at RAF Celle in Germany.
	21st July	Fg Off Forrest promoted to Squadron Leader and took command.
1953	January	Good flying conditions, poor aircraft serviceability. Four aircraft at RAF Turnhouse for monthly Sector exercise.
	May	Rehearsals for Queen's flypast over Hampden Park. 602 required to move from their normal dispersal at Renfrew due to building programme for the new civil terminal.
	June	Flypast for Queen over Hampden Park.
	July	Annual camp RAF Tangmere. Sqn Ldr R B Davidson DFC in command. (A former Auxiliary, but now a regular RAF Officer).
	August	During Exercise 'Momentum' Flt Lt Stuart Robinson suffered a flame-out in his Vampire. With the assistance of Jack Daly in an accompanying Vampire, he made a successful "dead stick" landing 70 miles away at Leuchars receiving a subsequent "Good Show" from the AOC-in-C Fighter Command.
1954	January	Good month, exercise at RAF Dyce—another 'Wing-Ding'. More planned, good for morale! "Seven aircraft airborne over Glasgow, first time for some months that a formation of any size has displayed the 'hidden talent' to Glaswegians".
	February	In spite of weather, 602 topped other Scottish Auxiliary Squadrons for flying hours.
	March	Sergeants' Mess moved into Abbotsburn House.
	18th June	Move back to RNAS Abbotsinch completed.
	September	Plt Off Philip joined 602 for the remainder of his National Service Committment after which he re-joined as an Auxiliary. "One of the most satisfactory features (of the Squadron) is the intake of younger pilots. At least 50% of the pilots are in thier early twenties which is a healthy sign for the Squadron's future."
	3rd October	Fg Off Hogg and Sergeant Watson successfully baled out of Meteor T7, WA629, over Perthshire "due to instrument failure".
	November	Changes announced in the running of Auxiliary Squadrons. They were no longer to be 1st line Squadrons but would become reserves behind the Regulars.
	December	Flying trophy presented to Fg Off J V P Daly.
1955	January/February	Smog! Typical Clyde Valley weather. Only 5½ days fit for flying during February.
	July	Annual camp at RAF Horsham St Faith. Visit by 602's Hon Air Commodore, The Duke of Hamilton, accompanied by his son Angus, then a CCF cadet.
	September	Annual Fighter Command Exercise 'Beware'. "Vampires unable to cope against high altitude attacks."
	November	Clyde Valley winter—only twelve flying days. 602 indulging in 'Rats and Terriers' exercises. "It would appear that one must fire inverted from 90° off to get an 'A' rating on Cine film these days."
	December	Flying Trophy to Fg Off A H Bowman. Airmen's Ball. Sergeants' Mess entertained Officers. Children's Party in Town HQ. "A good year without an avoidable accident".

1956	January	Training officer, Flt Lt R C (Ron) Bridges, received Queen's Commendation for Valuable Services in the Air. Ron had done much to improve the overall efficiency of the Squadron since his arrival in September 1953. Ball in Wardroom at Abbostinch attended by Caledonian Sector Commander plus four previous 602 COs—Group Captain Marcus Robinson, Wg Cdr H M Stephen, Wg Cdr J I Kilmartin and Sqn Ldr J A Forrest plus Naval and other guests.
	March	Vampire T11 borrowed from RAF Leuchars—"most useful".
	April	Announcement made that 602 Squadron has won the Cooper Trophy—awarded to the Auxiliary Squadron which had shown the greatest improvement.
	4th May	Sqn Ldr D C Bartman assumed command.
	May	Aircraft fitted with drop tanks and 6 pilots carried out long range "cross countries" of 640 miles to prepare for the long haul to annual camp at Gibraltar.
	23rd June	Presentation of Cooper Trophy at Abbotsinch by The Duke of Hamilton. Parade and fly-past.
	July	Annual camp, RAF North Front, Gibraltar. Detatchment to French Air Force base at Oran proposed but in the event four Mistrals (French built Vampires) visited 602 at Gibraltar.
	September	Air Defence Exercise "Stronghold".
	November	Kindly weather. Four new pilots. Vampire T11 delivered—a much more appropriate training aircraft than the Meteor for a Vampire Squadron. It might be wondered why it took so long for the single seat Vampire-equipped Squadrons to be supplied with the two-seat Vampire trainer. Twin-engined Meteors could not have been of any real value since they had of quite different flying characteristics. For the first time since the War the Squadron had a vacancy for two pilots.

	December	Flying ceased early as only 6½ days being suitable. However 602 achieved a post-war record by completing 2504 annual flying hours.
		Trophies awarded. Cine Flt Sgt J Watson
		                      Air to Air Fg Off W Winchester
		                      Flying Fg Off I E Hogg.
		Rumours abounded regarding future of Auxiliary Air Force flying Squadrons.

1957	January	In New Year's Honours List, 602's engineering officer, Flt Lt D B "Jock" MacFarlane BEM received the MBE. Signal received:— "All flying Squadrons of the Royal Auxiliary Air Force to be disbanded WEF 10th March 1957."
	23rd January	Final Dining-in night at Town HQ Coplaw Street when Group Captain Marcus Robinson was guest of honour.
	27th January	Final parade at RNAS Abbotsinch reviewed by The Duke of Hamilton.
	February/March	Aircraft delivered out to Maintenance Units: Vampires to 19MU St Athan, Meteors to 12MU Kirkbride.
	3rd March	The Royal Standard, originally awarded to 602 (City of Glasgow) Squadron on 18th January, was presented to the Squadron at Coplaw Street and laid-up in Glasgow Cathedral immediately thereafter.

The final entry in the Operational Record Book states intriguingly—and sadly.

"Good feelings, not so good."
J I Walker
Flight Lieutenant
No 602 Squadron Royal Auxiliary Air Force
RNAS Abbotsinch.

THE POST-WAR ERA

In the aftermath of the War, the country faced immense economic problems in a changed social climate. The decision to reform the Auxiliary Air Force was announced by Mr John Strachey, Under Air Secretary in the newly elected Labour Government, early in 1946.

No better choice to lead the re-formed 602 at Abbotsinch could have been made than Marcus Robinson. He gladly dropped rank from that of Group Captain, which he had attained during the War, to do so. He was not alone as a number of other pilots cheerfully relinquished their previous commissions to join the limited establishment as NCO aircrew. Some were subsequently recommissioned.

Of the pre-war 602, Donald Jack and Dunlop Urie returned to help the CO recreate the Squadron. Archie Robinson, agricultural auctioneer, with a DFC won with the Pathfinders, became Flight Commander and took charge of the Pipe Band. The nucleus of the post-war 602 began to gather—Jack Forrest NCO pilot who was to become CO in 1952, Johnny Lake, Bill Melling, Paul Reid, and student architect Alex Richardson, along with accountant Ivor Reid and Hamish McWilliam who were 602's only fatalities during the post-war period. They were joined by big Bill MacGregor who became Flight Commander and surveyor Jim Johnston, who was 602's last Flight Commander. Jack Laird and Ian 'Boy' Paxton and a quartet that seem to go naturally together, Alex Bowman, superb fighter pilot, Jack Daly ex Spitfires and Hornets with 19 Squadron whose experiences with the Gestapo and as a POW would make another story, Ian Hogg, who became a Captain with Singapore Airways and Johnny ('Horse', from his laugh) McGuire a Glasgow fruit merchant, together with Tom Wright a pilot with British European Airways.

They were supported, as always, by the ground crews including Bill McKinnon and Flt Sgt Harry Henderson who had joined in 1931 and served right to the end in 1957 to become the Squadron's most senior NCO.

Two of 602's real characters could not be kept away, the Reverend Lewis Sutherland, Minister of the Church of the Holy Rude, Stirling and 602's Padre from the thirties and Glen Niven, one of the 'Few' who had resisted attempts to post him to any other squadron, but who had been invalided out came back as civilian secretary. Robin Reid spent some time as Auxiliary Adjutant to be replaced by A W 'Birkie' Brown for whom Intelligence was another responsibility. 'Doc' Stewart became Medical Officer.

Marcus Robinson lost no time in getting 602 airborne again with the first aircraft, a Harvard trainer arriving during August 1946 to be followed with the first Spitfire, a FR Mk14, coming in October. The Squadron was to be equipped, for operational purposes, with Spitfire F21s and a few 14s for training—at least that was the official intention.

Training in the air began from Abbotsinch, now the Royal Naval Air Station HMS Sanderling, and, on the ground, at the Town HQ 49 Coplaw Street. The first post-war summer camp being held at RAF Woodvale during the Glasgow 'Fair', July 1947. Flying was largely carried out at weekends though it was possible on some weekdays and on summer evenings.

The Griffon engined Spitfires were none too popular being nearly twice the weight of the original Mark Is with twice the power. They were heavy and stiff with take-off and landing needing a deft touch to overcome the torque and a tendency to swing—"the wings wanted to go round the engine". By the end of 1948 the elegant Mark 22 had appeared replacing the 14s with more of them coming from other auxiliary squadrons during 1950 as 602 waited impatiently for jets.

During 1948 the Russian blockade of Berlin began with that City being supplied by air alone and the 'cold war' became hot in June 1950 with the outbreak of the conflict in Korea. During March 1949, 602 participated in large scale air defence exercises over the Forth/Clyde area. By then, Jim Johnston had showed his mettle by force-landing his Spitfire F21 near Coatbridge after engine failure. The pilots' notes for this aircraft did not encourage this course of action!

Marcus Robinson handed over command to Harborne Stephen during September 1950 thus completing a remarkable record of service beginning with his commission into the Auxiliiary Air Force in 1934. He wasn't lost completely as he became the first airman to become Chairman of the local Territorial Association, 602's immediate administrative controlling authority. H M Stephen, DSO DFC and Bar had been a distinguished fighter pilot during the war, notably with 74 Squadron. He was an executive with Beaverbrook Newspapers in Glasgow and later became Managing Director of the Daily Telegraph in London. Under him, 602 made the easy transition to jets in January 1951. The Vampire, with which they were re-equipped, was a delight to fly, no swing, no torque, excellent visibility—"a real kiddie car". The transition was made at Renfrew, Glasgow's civil airport where 602 had moved in June 1949. Consideration had been given to moving to Prestwick, a better proposition operationally and with Squadron associations through its early development by two ex CO's, the Duke of Hamilton and David McIntyre. Then, as now, the distance from Glasgow was a powerful deterrent and Renfrew, extended and with proper runways built during the war, proved adequate for the new jets.

In view of the tense international situation it was decided to mobilise the auxiliary flying squadrons for a period of three months continuous training. For 602 this meant moving to RAF Leuchars to train alongside the regular 43 and 222 Squadrons. Clearly it was time well spent, professionally and socially, achieving record flying hours. During the visit by Air Marshal Sir Basil Embry, AOC in C Fighter Command, Jack Daly suffered a flame-out from an engine which had only twelve hours on the clock. He made a skilful dead-stick landing on the airfield with minimal damage all round. It proved the sceptics wrong about the Vampire's characteristics in such circumstances and may have given an added piquancy to the pep-talk which Sir Basil was delivering to the assembled 602 at the time! On another gin clear still day, a perfect figure of eight was described in contrails over Fife. The opportunity was too good to miss however and it wasn't long before a vulgar addition had been made. The fact that it was fifteen miles long ensured that the subsequent irate phone calls came from the Highlands to the Borders!

602 returned to Renfrew in July 1951 to find it occupied by USAF F-84 Thunderjets, which had been delivered by the old wartime route of ship to Glasgow's King George V Dock and thence by a short road journey to Renfrew for preparation and onward air delivery. (A few years previously USAF F-80 Shooting Stars had been delivered to Europe in a similar way.) Eventually, 602 regained their Bessoneau hangars and dispersal beside the Lockheed hangars and the Vampires, the two Meteor 7s and, for a short while still, two Harvards became familiar sights and sounds over Clydeside. The training continued from Renfrew, interrupted at times by low aircraft serviceability and the often poor weather of the West of Scotland. Battle climbs, formations, rats and terriers (the interception of low flying raiders), practice interceptions and air-to-air firing became the pilot's staple diet punctuated by 'Wing Dings' when all three Scottish Auxiliary Fighter Squadrons would operate together, usually from Turnhouse, under the Scottish Auxiliary Wing Leader.

The obsolescence of the Vampire became increasingly obvious. In November 1951 the swept-wing F-86 Sabres of 410 Squadron Royal Canadian Air Force had been shipped to the Clyde aboard HMCS Magnificent and prepared at Renfrew. Beside them, even then, the Vampires looked rather ancient.

Jack Forrest took over command from 'Steve' in 1952 and was to be 602's last auxiliary CO. It was a lot to ask of anyone who also had a full-time job to do. For their 1952 annual camp 602 went to RAF Celle in Germany and in October participated in Exercise 'Ardent', the largest air defence exercise since the war. 1953 saw the Coronation of the Queen in July and 602 along with 603 and 612 Squadrons performed a flypast during her visit to Hampden Park in Glasgow. Camp that year was at RAF Tangmere, and with the resident No. 1 (Fighter) Squadron temporarily away, 602 borrowed one of their prize possessions, a top hat liberated from a Claridges doorman. 1 Squadron, on their return, retaliated by painting one of the 602 Vampires in 1 Squadron markings!

With Jack Forrest's move to the Middle East, Squadron Leader R B 'Bert' Davidson DFC, sometime member of 603 and a regular officer, took command in October 1953. The Vampires began to be camouflaged early in 1954 though it didn't help them much when it came to intercepting the bombers during the Autumn exercises. Jim Watson and Ian Hogg successfully baled-out from one of the Meteors after suffering instrument failure, the Meteor making a large hole in the Cromlix Estate, where Jim and Ian were duly entertained by the owner, Lady Eden. National Service pilots were now beginning to join the Squadron, among them Ken McKay, R A D Philip, K J Rosenfield, P B Lockwood, W Fletcher, P B Bell, S M Middleton and A G R Caie. Morale was excellent given the aged equipment though thè auxiliaries were now regarded as a purely reserve force. Social life continued at the Town HQ and at Abbotsburn House near Abbotsinch. Relations with their fellows in the Scottish Air Division, RNVR at Abbotsinch were excellent both in the air and in the Wardroom. After protracted negotiations with the Royal Navy, 602 moved back to Abbotsinch during June 1954. The building of the new terminal buildings at Renfrew on 602's dispersal had already forced them to move back to Renfrew's original hangar area. During September 1955 602 were active participants in exercise 'Beware'. The Vampires were unable to intercept the bombers though Al Bowman had managed to bag a B-45 Tornado. A new air firing range on the West Coast was due to become operational early in the New Year which would help 602's training.

In May 1956, Squadron Leader C D 'Don' Bartman became CO in time to receive the Cooper Trophy, awarded to 602 as the Squadron making the greatest improvement in overall efficiency. This was presented at Abbotsinch on Saturday 23rd June by 602's Honorary Air Commodore, His Grace the Duke of Hamilton. In July, after some test endurance flying, the squadron went to Gibraltar for their annual camp.

Clearly the matter of re-equipment was urgent. There would seem to have been plans to give all the auxiliaries Hunters and one had already been demonstrated to the Scottish Auxiliary Wing at Turnhouse. Rumours were none the less beginning to circulate about disbandment.

The abortive Suez Campaign of November 1956 was a prelude to the blow which fell suddenly on Sunday 6th January 1957.

By signal, all flying was cancelled with immediate effect to avoid any last minute wrecklessness, and the flying squadrons of the Royal Auxiliary Air Force were to be disbanded by 10th March. Whatever was said, rather insultingly, about the inability of the auxiliaries to fly and maintain modern high performance aircraft it was a plain and simple matter of money in the face of which no amount of skill, commitment, courage, and value could prevail. The Air National Guard in the US manages to fly the latest jets often from municipal airports, and even beat the regulars in competition. 602 and its fellow Auxiliary Squadrons could have done likewise if the political vision and will had been there.

All communications should be addressed to
The Secretary,
Territorial and Auxiliary Forces Association,
75 Berkeley Street,
Glasgow, C.3.

TERRITORIAL AND AUXILIARY FORCES
ASSOCIATION OF THE COUNTY OF
THE CITY OF GLASGOW

Ref.

FC/S.46415/Org.

FIGHTER COMMAND ADMINISTRATIVE INSTRUCTION NO. 5/57.
DISBANDMENT OF ROYAL AUXILIARY AIR FORCE SQUADRONS IN FIGHTER COMMAND.

1. Authority has been given in Air Ministry letter C.76735/55/S.9/
293 dated 16th January, 1957, for the disbandment of the following
Royal Auxiliary Air Force Squadrons in Fighter Command.

NO. 602 (CITY OF GLASGOW) SQUADRON R. AUX.A.F. -
R.N.A.S. ABBOTSINCH

INTENTION.

2. To disband all Royal Auxiliary Air Force Squadrons im Fighter
Command.

EXECUTION.

3. All action to effect the disbandment of Royal Auxiliary Air
Force Squadrons in Fighter Command is to be completed by not later
than 10th March, 1957.

(Sgd) A.E. LOWE
Group Captain
For Air Officer Commanding-in-Chief
Fighter Command

Bentley Priory,
30th January, 1957.

CERTIFIED TRUE EXTRACT

Assistant Secretary

Glasgow Territorial & Auxiliary Forces Association.

4th August, 1965.

There remained the final parades, and the presentation and laying-up of the Royal Standard, authorised by King George VI away back in 1952. This ceremony duly took place at Coplaw Street on Sunday 3rd March 1957 with the Standard being laid-up in Glasgow Cathedral immediately thereafter. The final parade had taken place at Abbotsinch on Sunday 27th January and the aircraft ferried away during February and March.

Among the regular RAF Officers who followed Cunliffe and Jackson were John Muir from Larkhall who went on to fly with 43 Squadron and Aer Lingus. Angus Maxwell ex Typhoons, Ted Griffin seconded from 222 Squadron, Messrs Powell and Johnson, 'Hank' Costain, Ray McPhie, who, transferring to Bomber Command, went on to command 100 Squadron and become chief pilot instructor at the Gaydon 'V' Bomber base, and R C 'Ron' Bridges. Ron McGowan and J I 'Johnny' Walker complete the list.

Responsible for the aircraft were successively the engineering officers, Hume, Beedie, Gough, Logan, 'Tommy' Barron and D B 'Donny' MacFarlane the latter receiving the MBE.

Among the auxiliary ground staff were the armament officers Flt Lt Stan Hillson and Flying Officers McAllister and McLean and, keeping the books, was John Bowd. Ken Askins, a qualified pilot, was auxiliary engineering officer for a short period and the Reverend D Noel Fisher of Sherbrooke Church Glasgow replaced the much loved Lewis Sutherland as padre in 1953.

The City of Glasgow didn't pay much attention to its Fighter Squadron after the war. It took Bill McConnell and his cadets in No.2175 (Rolls-Royce) Squadron Air Training Corps, to build a Museum and organise an Association dedicated to the memory of 602. Their achievement is splendid and the Museum at Hillington, opened by Marshal of the Royal Air Force Lord Cameron on Saturday 22nd October 1983, a fitting memorial to a remarkable institution.

The 60th anniversary of the founding of 602 Squadron was celebrated at a civic reception in Glasgow City Chambers and afterwards the Museum at Hillington on Friday 13th September 1985. A further memorial is the Spitfire F21, LA198, which served with 602 from 1947 to 1949 as RAI-G. It returned to Scotland from RAF Locking early in 1986 and was carefully restored and repainted in its 602 markings by RAF Leuchars to be displayed as the Station's Gate Guardian.

Should the need ever arise again, the spirit of 602 could be re-kindled and the immortal inspiration of the legend be employed in the defence of our country.

NOTABLE ACHIEVEMENTS

- First Auxilary Squadron to be formed.
- First to win Auxiliary Air Force Trophy in 1929.
- First to introduce the kilt, (in 1937) and to wear Highland mess kit.
- First Auxiliary Squadron to be equipped with the Spitfire—ahead of many regular RAF Squadrons in May 1939.
- Shot down the first enemy aircraft over the U.K. during World War II on 16th October 1939 and first enemy aircraft over U.K. soil, 28th October 1939.
- Wartime tally of enemy aircraft shot-down by VE Day. 150 enemy aircraft destroyed including 89 in the Battle of Britain.

"It has been written of them that they had a curious blend of courage and blind faith in the superiority of their aircraft and their own fighting ability".

GP. CAPT. D F McINTYRE AFC.

The others . . . to their skill and dedication

In the immediate post-war world, the fighter squadrons of the Auxiliary Air Force, 602 (City of Glasgow), 603 (City of Edinburgh) and 612 (County of Aberdeen), were not the only 'week-end' fliers. Air Observation Post Squadrons were formed from May 1949. The Scottish one, No.666, had its Headquarters at Scone and detached Flights at RAF Turnhouse and RNAS Abbostinch—the latter being originally intended for RAF Dyce.

666 Squadron and its flights—
No.1966 at Scone
No.1967 at RNAS Abbotsinch (initially at Renfrew)
No.1968 at RAF Turnhouse

They were part of the Royal Auxiliary Air Force though their Officers, were Territorial Army.

The RAF Volunteer Reserve also flourished with 11 Reserve Flying School at Scone and, for a short period, 13 RFS at Grangemouth together with the University Air Squadrons of Glasgow, Edinburgh, St Andrews and Aberdeen. All were administered by 66 (Scottish) Reserve Group as were the Auxiliary Air Force Squadrons until their transfer to Fighter Command on 1st November 1949.

The Royal Navy inaugurated an Air Branch of the RNVR from May 1947, when 1830 Squadron was based at RNAS Abbotsinch alongside 602 Squadron. In 1952 it was expanded and the Scottish Air Division came into being incorporating 1830 Squadron, and its off-shoot 1830A, which later became 1843 Squadron.

The Reserve Flying Schools were disbanded during 1952 although 11RFS remained in being until 1954 and all the flying squadrons of the Royal Auxiliary Air Force and Royal Navy Volunteer Reserve were disbanded by 10th March 1957.

The University Air Squadrons of Glasgow and Strathclyde, East Lowlands and Aberdeen, Dundee and St Andrews continue and with the Volunteer Glider Schools, 661 at Kirknewton, 662 at Arbroath and 663 at Kinloss, together with No. 12 Air Experience Flight at Turnhouse currently serve the needs of the Air Training Corps and Combined Cadet Forces.

The Auxiliary tradition did continue in Scotland after March 1957, though not in the flying roles, notably with 2 Maritime HQ Unit at Pitreavie with its Town HQ at 603's old quarters at Learmonth Terrace, Edinburgh.

Alongside 602 Squadron were 2602 Squadron Royal Auxiliary Air Force Regiment for airfield defence duties and 3602 Squadron Fighter Control Unit. Both were based at RAF Bishopbriggs near Glasgow. The Edinburgh and Aberdeen Squadrons were likewise supported by 2603 & 3603 and 2612 & 3612.

During the war additional Auxiliary Air Force Squadrons were formed for Balloon Barrage defence. In Glasgow these were numbered 945, 946 and 947 Squadrons.

AN ELITE
THE PRE-WAR SQUADRON

First parade in uniform—Renfrew, March 1926. In the background can be seen Arkleston Cemetery and the line of trees which still flank the M8 Motorway!

from the Marquess of Douglas and Clydesdale's log-book 1929.

1929 Date and Hour	Pilot	Machine Type and No.	Passenger	Time	Height	Course	Remarks
12 July	Self	Fawn	LAC Murray	1·00	3000	Renfrew - Leuchars	Squadron Formation X County
13 "	"	7769	P/o Buch	20			Formation Dual
"	"	"	P/o Lloyd	20		"	" Dual
"	"	"	P/o Buch	30			Forced landing Dual
"	"	"	P/o Lloyd	30		"	" Dual
"	"	"	"	40			Dual.
"	"	7185	LAC Tait		4000	Leuchars - Turnhouse	X Country
"	"	"	"	3·25		T - Scotland	X Country
16 "	"	"	7185	15	6000	S - Turnhouse	X Country
"	"	"	"	30		T - Leuchars	X Country
18 "	"	7212	AC Leake	10			Flying Efficiency Test
"	"	"	AC Brown	20			Formation
"	"	"	"	20			Formation
"	"	"	LAC Woods	35			Bombing
"	"	7769	P/o Murray	1·05		Leuchars - Montrose	Bombing Raid. Attack by 56(F) Sqdn.

Renfrew airport in its original form as a grass flying field in the late 1920s. The road which runs from left to right was shortened just past the line of hangars when the airfield was extended and runways laid down in 1943. It was operated by the Scottish Flying Club for the local authority.

Flooding at Renfrew—a problem to which it was prone.

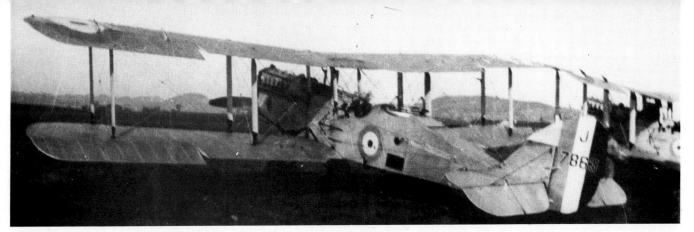

DH9A light bomber J7863 at Renfrew. The first type of aircraft to be flown by 602, between 1925 and 1927.

DH9As and the first issue of Lynx Avros (504Ns) at Leuchars during the annual camp, July 1927.

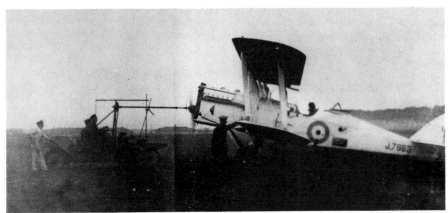

J P 'Bobby' Drew, one of 602's first three auxiliary pilots. (Killed, 28 May 1928).

DH9A being started by a Hucks starter at RAF Leuchars, during annual camp, July 1927.

Avro 504N, J9705 at Renfrew.

Sqn Ldr C N Lowe, MC, DFC, regular RAF— the first CO of 602 Squadron—September 1925. He later commanded 1 Squadron in 1926 and 43 Squadron in 1928.

Full dress uniform
Flt Lt McIntyre, Fg Off McNab, ?, early 1930s.

Oops!
Avro 504N, J9253 at Renfrew.

Sqn Ldr J Latta, MC, 602's first
Auxiliary CO, February 1926.

H M King George V opens the
Squadron's new town HQ at 49 Coplaw
Street, Glasgow, on 12th July 1927.

Fawn II, J7229.

Regular and Auxiliary Officers in front of a Fairey Fawn at annual camp, Leuchars 1928.
Sqn Ldr Fullerton is fourth from the right in the front row and Flt Lt Dan Martyn (first regular adjutant), is third from right.

David Lloyd and Assistant Adjutant Griffith Powell deliver urgently required medicine to Islay on 1st August 1930 in Avro 504N J9705. This was the first aircraft to land on the island and a precursor to the Scottish Air Ambulance Service.

D F McIntyre flying Fawn J7190.

Wapiti J9094 and J9602 'making love'.
At Leuchars during annual camp, 29th
July 1930.

Wapiti, J9862 over Renfrewshire, early 1930s.

Avro 504N, H2975 after a mid-air collision with Wapiti J9603, in which Plt Off Phillips was killed, 7th March 1931.

Wreckage of Wapiti J9603 which came down two miles from Port Glasgow after colliding with the above Avro 504N. Plt Off Harold Land was killed but his observer/gunner A/C Eddie Smith parachuted to safety.

Wapiti trainer K2239 at Renfrew with a Hucks starter, 1932.

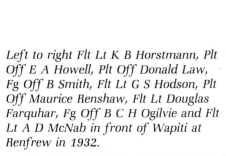

Left to right Flt Lt K B Horstmann, Plt Off E A Howell, Plt Off Donald Law, Fg Off B Smith, Flt Lt G S Hodson, Plt Off Maurice Renshaw, Flt Lt Douglas Farquhar, Fg Off B C H Ogilvie and Flt Lt A D McNab in front of Wapiti at Renfrew in 1932.

Starting an Avro 504N with Assistant Adjutant 'Stacey' Hodson, and Edward Howell.

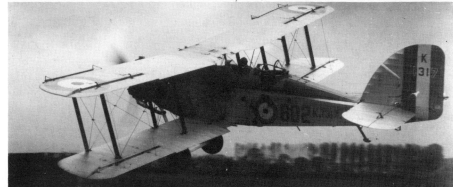

Wapiti at Renfrew in 1932 flying over what is now the M8 motorway. The line of trees still exists.

Wapitis at Abbotsinch—newly opened in 1933.

The Scottish Auxiliary Rugby Team, 1932—they beat the Hendon squadrons in that and subsequent years!

First Pipe Band parade, 1933. Formed from the complete band of the 6th Paisley Company of the Boys' Brigade whose members were all aged 16 and too old to continue in the BB. They happily accepted the Marquess of Douglas and Clydesdale's invitation to join 602.

Accident at Lympne, Avro 504N, K1983. 24th July 1934.

Scottish Aviation Ltd, Prestwick. (Incorporated 9th August 1935). Prestwick Airport opened as a grass field on 17th February 1936. Both were inspired and developed by D F McIntyre with the Marquess of Douglas and Clydesdale, later Duke of Hamilton (both 602 Squadron COs).

SCOTTISH AVIATION
LTD

Hart, K3044 over Argyllshire

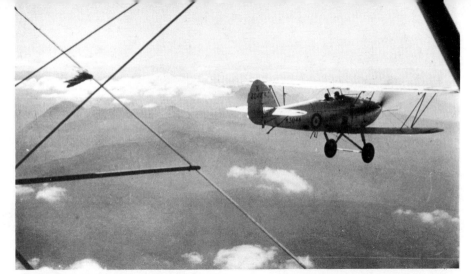

'A' Flight Hawker Hart, K3862 at Abbotsinch in 1934.

'B' Flight Hart at Abbotsinch in 1934. The tenements in background remain to this day.

Hawker Harts of 602 Squadron over the '534', which became the 'Queen Mary', at John Brown's, Clydebank, 1934.

Harts near Loch Lomond 1935

RAF Abbotsinch, 1936. The Inchinnan Road and tenements at Douglas Terrace which are still in use can be seen on the right.

602 Squadron, annual camp at RAF Tangmere, July 1936.
Back row: Messrs. Urie, Pinkerton, Boyd, Johnstone, Robinson, Bell, McLean, ?, Ferguson, Muspratt-Williams.
Front-row: Rintoul, ?, Farquhar, Clydesdale, (CO), ?, Selway (Adj), Feather, ?, Grant.

Hawker Hinds at Abbotsinch, 1937.

602 Squadron, annual camp at Rochford (Southend) July 1937. Picture taken to celebrate the granting of permission for Auxiliary Officers to wear the kilt.

Oops!
Fg Off J Hawkes in Hind K5510 during annual camp at Rochford, 27th July 1937.

Empire Air Day 1937? One of 602's Avro Tutors, K3305.

Vivian Bell in Hind leaving Inverness having dropped-off Alistair Grant. Note large '602' in red and official rendering of badge on fin.

Donald Jack flying Hind K5511, 1937.

The original 602 Squadron badge (based upon the City of Glasgow coat of arms).

The official Squadron badge as approved by King George VI in 1937

602, 'Bomber' Squadron Hind showing application of official badge—the crossed-lion within the bomber squadron's grenade.

Annual camp at RAF Church Fenton, July 1939.
Cpl. Jeffrey i/c Guard.

Flt Lt George Pinkerton with 602
Squadron Gauntlet LO-K, probably
K7879. This picture was taken during
May 1939 at Abbotsinch and
demonstrates that the first code letters
for 602 were in fact the familiar 'LO', to
be replaced by 'ZT' on the Spitfires
initially, and reverting to 'LO' just prior
to the outbreak of war. A very rare
photograph!

Oops!
Spitfire I, ZT-P on her nose during
annual camp RAF Church Fenton, July
1939.

No photographs exist of 602 Squadron Hawker Hectors. They were only on charge for a short period and were not very popular.
The type is shown here in a line-up of 612 (County of Aberdeen) Squadron's aircraft at Dyce in 1937/38.

Muspratt-Williams, Ferguson, McKellar and Padre Sutherland, Annual camp, July 1939, RAF Church Fenton.

56

Paul Webb, flying Spitfire I ZT-N—
photo taken by Archie McKellar, 1939.

JULY - 1939.		NO	FLYING THIS MONTH.					
AUGUST - 1939.								
19-8-39	11.3c	Magister. L8161	P/O. Charrett.	self.	Abbotsinch : Flying practice on war type.	.15	2000
"	11.45	" "	self	—	" First solo on monoplanes.	.40	3000
"	17.2a	Tutor. K6097	"	P/O. Stone.	" Flying practice. etc.	.20	5000
27-8-39	12.45	Magister. L8161	"	—	" " 5 landings.	1.10.	1000.
29-8-39	17.05	Spitfire. K9965	"	—	" First solo on Spitfires, 2 landings.	.45	4000
30-8-39	15.10	" K9961	"	—	" Flying practice. 4 landings. Total for month	.45 (3.55)	8000
SEPTEMBER - 1939.								
3-9-39	—	—	WAR DECLAIRED ON		GERMANY. ———		
6-9-39	12.25	Spitfire K9962	self.	—	Abbotsinch : Demonstration of Nos 1 & 2 attacks	.50	3000
8-9-39	11.10	" K9974	"	—	" Practicing No 1 + 2 attacks.	.35	3000
11-9-39	10.20	" K9962	"	—	" " "	.35	4000
12-9-39	19.55	" L1040	"	—	" First solo night flying. Carry forward	.05 (2.05)	1000
					TOTAL TIME ...	384.45 383.55	
						316.35	

From Alistair Grant's log-book 1939

Spitfire Is of 602 at Abbotsinch.

THE CHALLENGE OF WAR

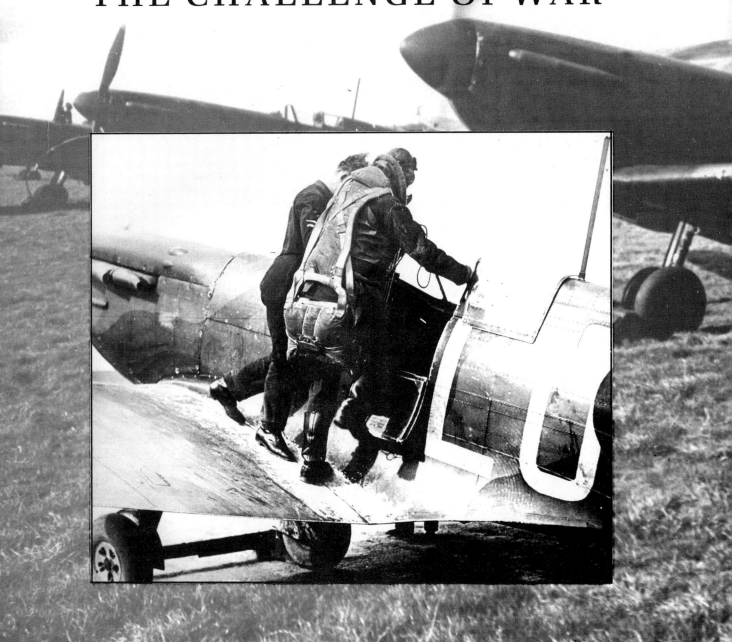

PREVIOUS PAGE:

Drem, March 1940

The immortal Spitfire
Flying Officers Alistair Grant and Hector MacLean in front of LO-D at Abbotsinch, just before the outbreak of the War, 1939.

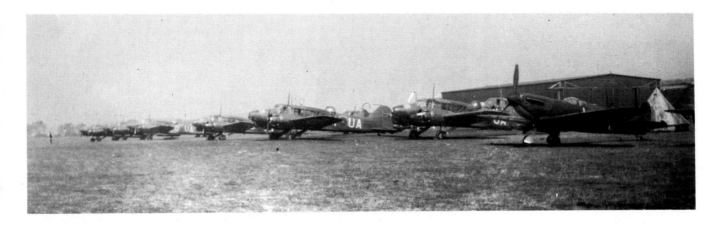

Spitfires of 602 Squadron and Ansons of 269 Squadron at
Abbotsinch, late August 1939.

*Spitfire Is at Abbotsinch, 1939.
K9970, LO-D in foreground.*

*602 Squadron Finlay Boyd and 'Marco'
Abbotsinch, 1939.*

*Muspratt-Williams and Marcus
Robinson with pups at Abbotsinch,
September 1939.*

Alastair Grant and pup with Spitfire I,
L1040, LO-E at Drem, October 1939.

Heinkel 111 shot down near Humbie in
the Lammermuir Hills on 28th October
1939 by the combined efforts of 602
and 603, the Glasgow and Edinburgh
Auxiliary Squadrons. It was the first
enemy aircraft to be brought down on
British soil in World War II and was
credited to Archie McKellar of 602.
Two panels from the Heinkel started
off the 602 Museum at Hillington
which opened in October 1984.

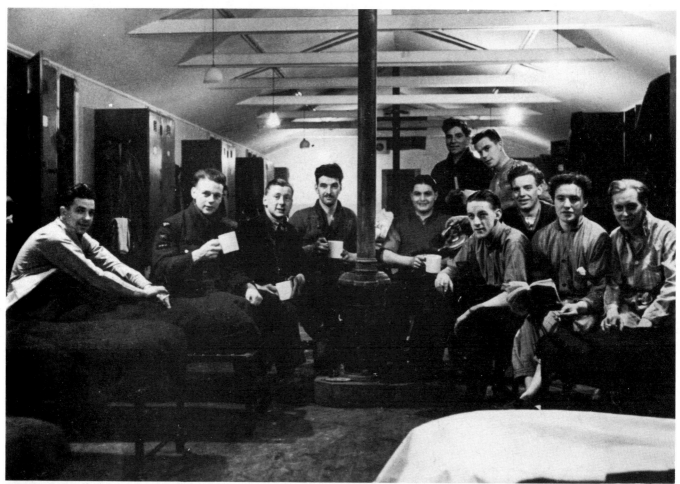

Some of the lads, just after call-up at Drem, 1939.

602's Spitfire Is at Grangemouth, October 1939.

Calm before the storm.
Left to right: Dunlop Urie, Alastair Grant, Norman Stone and Donald Jack play tenequoits at Abbotsinch.

602 Squadrom at Drem, October 1939.
Left to right: Finlay Boyd, George Pinkerton, Sandy Johnstone, Paul Webb, Alastair Grant and Nigel Graeme

Hector MacLean at Drem, October 1939.

Christmas Dinner, Drem 1939.

Probably CO Douglas Farquhar's original aircraft at Drem 1939, K9962.

Sgt Andy MacDowall at Drem, March 1940. 'Mac' was subsequently commissioned and eventually commanded the RAF's first Meteor jet squadron, 616 at the end of the War.

"Stevie with his creation on LO-D. Driver, Flt Lt Dunlop Urie."
Named after a sortie when abortive radar directions caused this pilot to turn in ever decreasing circles and nearly disappeared like the Ogu-Pogu bird up his own . . .

Ian Ferguson and Glyn Ritchie at Drem 1940.

Avro Tutor, K6097, Abbotsinch Station Flight, possibly used by 602. Abbotsinch, January 1940

"Our Magister" 602's L8161 at Abbotsinch, January 1940.

N2102 Fairey Battle of 602 Squadron at Abbotsinch in January 1940. The two Battles N2102 and N2103 were used as an introduction to the Spitfire.

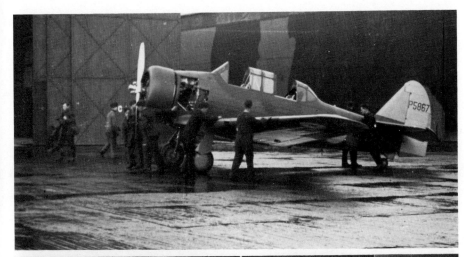

602's Harvard 1 at Drem, 1940

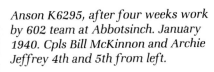

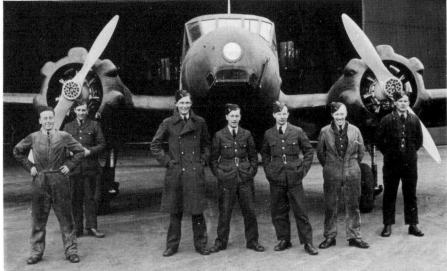

Anson K6295, after four weeks work by 602 team at Abbotsinch. January 1940. Cpls Bill McKinnon and Archie Jeffrey 4th and 5th from left.

Winter, Drem, 19th January 1940, ex Imperial Airways HP42 class G-AAXC, "Hanno".

602 at Drem, early 1940.

After decorating Sqn Ldr A D Farquhar with the DFC, H M King George VI meets other Squadron pilots at Drem. Left to right: Air Marshal Dowding (C in C Fighter Command), Gp Capt Charles Keary (Station Commander), Sqn Ldr Farquhar, (CO 602 Squadron), King George VI, Marcus Robinson, Sandy Johnstone, Wheeldon and George Proudman. 26th February 1940.

Refuelling at Dyce, early 1940.

Drem, early 1940.
Note cannon-armed Spitfire Ia at left.
Presumably L1007 on trials with 602.

*"The CO's Kite," LO-A
at Drem early 1940.*

*Patrolling over East Coast. Spitfire Ia;
N3109, LO-J.*

*Spitfire Ia; K9910, LO-G after forced-
landing.*

Spitfire Ia; K9964, LO-B, 'Bogus' at Drem, 19th March 1940.

Left to right: Donald Jack, Archie McKellar, 'Roger' Coverley, Glyn Ritchie, Paul Webb and Ian Ferguson at Drem 1940.

Crew room at Drem, March 1940. Left to right: Donald Jack, Nigel Graeme, Archie McKellar (lying down), Cyril Babbage and Hector MacLean.

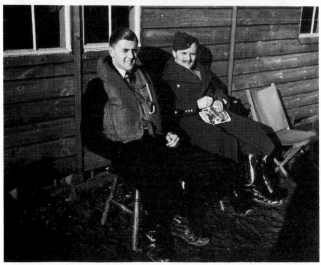

Sandy Johnstone and Archie McKellar at Drem 1940

"What General Weygand called the Battle of France is over. I expect that the Battle of Britain is about to begin. The whole fury and might of the enemy must very soon be turned on us. Hitler knows that he will have to break us in this island or lose the War. If we can stand up to him, all Europe may be free and the life of the world may move forward into broad sunlit uplands. But, if we fail, then the whole world, including the United States, including all that we have known and cared for, will sink into the abyss of a new Dark Age made more sinister, and perhaps more protracted, by the lights of perverted science. Let us therefore brace ourselves to our duties, and so bear ourselves that, if the British Empire and its Commonwealth last for a thousand years, men will still say 'This was their finest hour'."

JULY 1940

"The gratitude of every home in our island, in our Empire, and indeed throughout the world, except in the abodes of the guilty, goes to the British airmen, who undaunted by odds, and unswerving in their constant challenge and mortal danger, are turning the tide of world war by their prowess and devotion. Never in the field of human conflict was so much owed by so many to so few."

20TH AUGUST 1940

WINSTON CHURCHILL

The grave of Archie McKellar, DSO, DFC with Bar in the New Eastwood Cemetery, Thornliebank.

Killed in action 1st November 1940 in the defence of London during the Battle of Britain.
'One of the few to whom so many owe so much.'

Archie McKellar exemplified in so many ways the finest qualities of Glasgow's fighter pilots—wiry, aggressive, highly skilled and a leader of men, possessed of charm, wit and a generous nature. He left 602 on promotion to 605 Squadron during 1940 and met his death whilst commanding it. Having downed a total of sixteen enemy aircraft during the Battle of Britain he missed by only eight hours inclusion in its Roll of Honour.

Alistair Grant, Archie McKellar and Paul Webb at Drem.

Alastair Grant's Spitfire 1a; K9899, LO-H at Drem 4th June 1940

During the Battle of Britain 602 Squadron, 'A' Flight dispersal at Westhampnett.

Contrails in the sky . . . during the Battle of Britain, summer 1940.

"The motto on one of our aircraft which the Squadron lived up to."

X4110 after Dunlop Urie must have created the record for the shortest operational life of a Spitfire—twenty minutes.
Spitfire X4110 had just been delivered to 602 at Westhampnett on the morning of the 18th August 1940 and was scrambled in the afternoon. Fortunately Dunlop Urie survived.

Without whom . . .
Left to right: G Sherlaw, T Moir, T Stevenson, W Sweet, G W Hutchison and Blind Flying Panel.

The ever welcome YMCA tea wagon, Westhampnett, summer 1940.

602 Squadron, 'B' Flight dispersal at Westhampnett during the Battle Britain.

After the Battle, 'G' at 15 minutes readiness. Westhampnett, December 1940.

Glen (Nuts) Niven, 1940

602 is rested after the Battle at Prestwick, probably early 1941.

During filming of a 'Yank in the RAF' at Prestwick 1941. Spitfire IAs. Note 602's HQ the 'Old Mill'.

Spitfire IIa,s at the new Heathfield aerodrome , adjacent to Prestwick, 1941. P8047, LO-L, 'The Malverns' in the foreground.

DH 60G Moth, X5114 (ex G-ACCW),
would seem to have been used by 602
while at Heathfield in 1941.

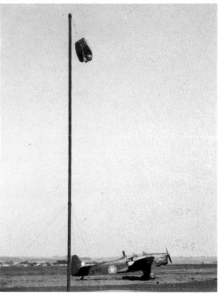

602's Magister R1915 at Heathfield
1941.
Note windsock—courtesy of WAAF!

*602 at Kenley 1941 under Sqn Ldr
Paddy Finucane, 4th from right.*

*Fitter, 'Buck' Harper, running up 'D' at
Kenley 1941.*

Spitfire Vb wearing 602's Lion Rampant! Kenley 1942.

Spitfire Vb "Hemel Hempstead" of 602 at Kenley, 1942.

Spitfire Vbs at Kenley 1942

Spitfires of 602 taxying out at Kenley 1942

Kenley 1942

602 at RAF Skeabrae in the Orkneys, 30th October 1942.
On front row l-r, Ralph Sampson, Eric Bocock, Mike Beytagh (CO), Johnny Niven and ?.

602 Squadron at Lasham April 1943.
Standing: Topham (IO), Osborne (MO),
Beytagh (CO), Freebourne (OC 'B' Flt),
Maggs (OC 'A' Flt), Aubertin, Loud, Guy,
Davey, and Strudwick.
Sitting: Kellers, Hannah, Penny, Parker,
Hargreaves, Willis, Noble, Blair and
Robson.

602 Squadron at Bognor July 1943.
Left to right: Bob Gourlay, Wooley,
Morgan, Ken Charney, Max Sutherland
(CO), Aubertin, Manson, Pierre
Clostermann, ?, ?, Roy Hook, 'Mac'
McConochie, Jimmy Kelly, Dumbrell.
On aircraft: Harry Cleary, ?, ?, Flt Sgt
Fox.

Spitfire VII, MD114 flown by Plt Off Ian
Blair DFM, of 602 Squadron at
Skeabrae. On 20th February 1944 he
shot-down a high flying Bf109F over the
Orkneys but due to parts of the 109
hitting his radiator he had to force land
on Stronsay.
NB: Code letters of previous user, 312
Squadron, remain. Colour scheme,
medium sea grey (upper) and PRU blue
(lower).

Spitfire IXb decorated by 602 at Detling 1944
with its Canadian and European complement of pilots.
Front row l-r: Aubertin, Max Sutherland, Bagget, Dumbrell, Spence, Jacques, Gourlay, Maggs, Hook, 'Chiefy' MacDonald.
Behind in front of nose l-r: Penny, Jenkins, Fox.
On wing l-r: Manson, Sorge, Robson, McConochie, Thomerson.
On fuselage l-r: Kistruck, Kelly, Charney, Wooley, Oste.
In cockpit: Clostermann (of 'Big Show' fame).

MH526, LO-D. Spitfire IXb of 602 Squadron at RAF Detling 1944.

602 at Antwerp, September 1944. First left rear, Raymond Baxter, second Roy Hook, fourth, Bob Stewart who had been CO temporarily after Chris le Roux's death.

602, in the fighter-bomber role with CO 'Max' Sutherland checking one of the 500lb bombs on his Spitfire LF XVIe, early 1945.

Raymond Baxter, briefs pilots before a strike, 1945. Tommy 'Cupid' Love from Rutherglen is third from the right.

602's pilots in front of a Spitfire LF XVIe shortly before the Squadron disbanded at Coltishall in May 1945.

602 Squadron at Coltishall 1945. Stan Sollitt and Cec Zuber in front of Spitfire LF XVIe SM3??, LO-J, Zuber's aircraft.

A lesser known aspect of the Auxiliary Air Force—City of Glasgow Balloon squadrons 945, 946 and 947 Squadron, Ian Blair's father, fourth from left.

From Flt Lt I R Sutherland's log-book at the end of the European War.

COLTISHALL

SINGLE-ENGINE AIRCRAFT				MULTI-ENGINE AIRCRAFT							PASSENGER	INSTR CLOUD FLYING [Incl. in cols. (1) to (10)]	
DAY		NIGHT		DAY			NIGHT						
Dual	Pilot	Dual	Pilot	Dual	1st Pilot	2nd Pilot	Dual	1st Pilot	2nd Pilot			Dual	Pilot
(1)	(2)	(3)	(4)	(5)	(6)	(7)	(8)	(9)	(10)	(11)		(12)	(13)
113/35	1583/35 1·30 ·10	5/00	107/35	1/20	16/00	4/30		00/40	3/55	43/50		21/40	28/30

MAY 8TH. VE DAY. JERRY PACKED HIS HAND INTODAY.

602 Glasgow Squadron Goes

Veterans of the Battle of Britain, the No. 602 (City of Glasgow) Squadron, one of the most famous fighter units in the R.A.F., has been disbanded, but may be reassembled as an auxiliary squadron with headquarters at Renfrew.

Sir Patrick Dollan, a life trustee of the squadron's benevolent fund, received intimation to this effect yesterday. The decision of the Air Ministry, he said, had come as a shock, and he trusted that West of Scotland M.P.s would raise the matter in Parliament, and insist on the decision being reconsidered.

The squadron had achieved remarkable successes in the Battle of Britain, the Battle of Germany, and in sweeps over Europe.

The original pilots were all volunteers who trained as auxiliaries at Renfrew on Saturday afternoons, and the squadron's "bag" of enemy 'planes is a large one. It was in action when the Luftwaffe raided the Firth of Forth early in the war, and many awards have been won by its airmen.

·20 ·15 ·20 ·30.

·20 ·15 ·20 ·30.

When we landed, G/Capt. Hawtry, Sector Commander told us that was our last trip as 602, and that the Squadron was being disbanded. So end the happiest days of my life!

/35	/00	/00	/35	1/20	16/25	4/30		00/40	3/55	43/00		21/40	25/30
(1)	(2)	(3)	(4)	(5)	(6)	(7)	(8)	(9)	(10)	(11)		(12)	(13)

PROBLEMS OF PEACE

PREVIOUS PAGE:

Press-day for the new Vampires at Renfrew: 27th January 1951. Harvards, still
with RAI markings, Spitfire 22 and BEA
Viking in background.

602 Squadron A.A.F.,
R.N.A.S. Abbotsinch.

Dear Lake

        I am at present filling seven
officer and eight Senior N.C.O. vacancies in this
Squadron and I am not entitled to hold officers
against the N.C.O. vacancies.

        You will appreciate that for
one reason or another all the best chaps sooner
or later gained commissions during the war and
nine out of ten applicants for 602 Squadron are
commissioned officers. I am therefore faced with
offering Senior N.C.O Vacancies to a number of
officers.

        If you feel that you are pre-
pared to resign your commission and accept cheerfully and enthusiastically such a position in 602
Squadron, I shall be glad to include you amongst
the successful aircrew applicants.

        Will you please let me have
your reply promptly.

                Yours sincerely,

                Marcus Robinson. S/Ldr.
        Commanding 602 Squadron A.A.F.

F/Lt. J. LAKE.
315 Clarkston Road
GLASGOW. S.2.

Sqn Ldr Marcus Robinson AFC.
First post-war Commanding Officer of
602 Squadron.

An invitation to join the Squadron from Marcus
Robinson to Johnny Lake who resigned his commission
in order to accept the offer.

Flt Sgt Jack Forrest and Sgts Mitchell and Reid with 602 Squadron Spitfire FR14E, probably TX985, RAI-B at Abbotsinch 1947.

Line-up of Spitfires at Abbotsinch, 1947.
Left to right: Mark FR14E, TP236 RAI-A (First Spitfire to be delivered to 602, post-war); F21s-LA225, RAI-J; LA193, RAI-E and RAI-H probably LA268 plus two others and three Harvard T2Bs likely to be FT141, KF374 and KF584.

First Annual camp, RAF Woodvale, July 1947 in front of Spitfire F21 LA198, RAI-G.
Back row: Yuille (accounts), Ivor Reid (killed during that camp), Hamish McWilliam, Hume (Regular
Engineer Officer), Jackson (Regular Assistant Adjutant), Alex Richardson and Archie Robinson.
Middle row: Joe Cunliffe (Regular Adjutant), Dunlop Urie, Marcus Robinson, Donald Jack and 'Doc' Stewart (MO).
Front row: Paul Reid, Johnny McGuire, Johnny Lake, Jack Forrest, Bill Melling and J Mitchell.

First Annual Summer Camp since reformation. RAF Woodvale, Glasgow Fair, July 1947.
Left to right: Jack Forrest, Bill Melling, Paul Reid, Ivor Reid, Hume (Eng. Officer),
Jackson (Regular Training Officer), Yuille (Accounts), Dunlop Urie, Marcus
Robinson (CO), Donald Jack, Cunliffe (Regular Adjutant), 'Doc' Stewart (MO),
Archie Robinson, Alex Richardson, Hamish McWilliam, Johnny McGuire, Johnny Lake and Johnny
Mitchell.

Aircraft:

LA198 RAI-G F21

TP 236 RAI-A FR14E   TX 985 RAI-B FR14E
LA268 RAI-H F21   LA211 RAI-K F21
LA 329 RAI-L F21   LA225 RAI-J F21
LA222 RAI-M F21   LA193 RAI-E F21

Messrs Urie, Jackson, Mitchell, Marcus Robinson, Forrest, Cunliffe, Ivor Reid and Richardson with Spitfire F21.

Marcus Robinson briefs his pilots, Sgts Mitchell and Melling with Fg Off Archie Robinson on the wing of Spitfore F21; LA222, RAI-M. 1947.

Sgts Bill Melling and Johnny Mitchell of 602.
One of a series of photographs taken of 602 whilst at their Woodvale camp in 1947
and used in the first post-war recruiting booklet for the Auxilary Air Force.
This one was used as a basis for the painting for the cover.

*'Pay parade' at Woodvale, July 1947.
Flt Lt Yuille pays out.*

Tea-up, Woodvale July 1947.

*602's original complement of NCO
pilots in front of Spitfire F21; LA222,
RAI-M. 1947.
Left to right: Sgts McGuire, Reid,
Mitchell, Melling, Forrest and Lake.*

*Jack Forrest taxying-out during annual
camp at Tangmere July 1947 in Spitfire
F21; LA 279, RAI-J.*

KF584, as RAI-X, one of 602's Harvard T2Bs in the all-over yellow training colour-scheme.

Spitfire F21; LA222, RAI-M having been successfully force-landed by Jim Johnston after engine failure near Glenboig on 31st October 1948. "I went over five hillocks and through three five-bar gates." The pilot's notes for the Spitfire 21 did not encourage attempts at forced-landings or ditchings!

YEAR		AIRCRAFT		PILOT, OR	2ND PILOT, PUPIL	DUTY
1948		TYPE	No.	1ST PILOT	OR PASSENGER	(INCLUDING RESULTS AND REMARKS)
MONTH	DATE					
—	—	—	—	⌐	—	— TOTALS BROUGHT FORWARD
OCT	17	SPITFIRE	F	SELF		FORMATION FLYING
"	18	HARVARD	141	SELF		N/F CIRCUITS
"	25	HARVARD	374	SELF		AEROBATICS N/F CIRCUIT
"	31	SPITFIRE	M	SELF		FLYING IN REDUCED VIS
						ENGINE FAILED. PRANGED
						AT GLENBOIG.
A.W. Robinson F/Lt						
a/c Flight						
Larson Robinson W/2		SUMMARY FOR OCT. 1948			SPITFIRE:	
		UNIT:- 602 R.AUX.A.F			HARVARD:	
		DATE:- 1st NOV. 1948				

From Jim Johnston's log-book showing the entry for October 31st 1948.

By yon bonny banks . . .

For 602's 1948 Christmas Card, a formation of four Spitfire 22s and two Sptifire 21s over Loch Lomond on 7th November 1948.
Left to right: PK 369, RAI-B; PK 349, RAI-D; LA198, RAI-G; PK560, RAI-C; PK578, RAI-A and LA275, RAI-H (the 21s being 'G' and 'H').

Spitfire F21; LA198, RAI-G, at Abbotsinch in early 1949. This aircraft guarded the gate at RAF Locking, but returned to Scotland during 1986 to be gate guardian at RAF Leuchars.
Jim Johnston also suffered an engine failure in this aircraft successfully landing it at RAF Horsham St Faith during 602's annual camp in July 1949. He ground-looped the aircraft intentionally to avoid an obstruction. It did not return to 602.

Spitfire F21, LA250, RAI-F at Renfrew on Saturday 2nd July 1949. The Squadron had just moved there from Abbotsinch where the steel tracking was in a poor state.
Initially they used the area near the fire station as shown here but soon moved to the dispersal area adjacent to the 'Lockheed' hangars.
Note the two Seafires.

AOC's inspection during annual camp at RAF Horsham St Faith, July 1949. In the background is a silver Spitfire 21, probably LA283 and further along Mark 22s of 603 Squadron including PK525, RAJ-M. The Edinburgh Squadron had preceded 602 at Horsham and must have lent themsome of their aircraft.

Another shot during the inspection at Horsham St Faith. A 602 Harvard and Spitfire 22; PK560, RAI-C in the background.

602's Pipe Band at Horsham St Faith during annual camp, July 1949.

Line-up at Horsham St Faith, camp July 1949.
Left to right: John Muir (Regular Adj), Archie Robinson, Bill Melling, Marcus Robinson (CO), Tom Wright, Duke of Hamilton, Bill MacGregor, Jack Forrest, Angus Maxwell, (Regular Training Officer), Gough (Regular Engineering Officer), Rev L A Sutherland, 'Doc' Stewart, (MO), and 'Birkie' Brown (Intelligence Officer).

Bill Melling, winner of air race at the
RAF Dyce Battle of Britain Show,
September 1949.
Spitfire F21, possibly LA319, RAI-G.

On parade!
Led by Sqn Ldr Marcus Robinson, 602
Squadron march past the Cenotaph in
George Square, Glasgow on Armistice
Day November 1949.

Bill Meldrum on wing, Bill Larkin in cockpit of Spitfire 21, 1949.

Jack Daly ready to go in Spitfire 21, LA269, LO-H. 1950.

Johnny McGuire preparing to fly in Spitfire F21 being assisted by Bill Larkin, 1950.

Cocktails . . .
Left to right: H M Stephen, Archie Robinson, Glen Niven, Stuart Robinson and Marcus Robinson—the 602 family Robinson! 'Steve' took command of 602 from Marcus Robinson in September 1950. He had had a very distinguished career as a fighter pilot with 74 Squadron during the Battle of Britain winning the DSO and two DFCs.

Is this Marcus Robinson handing over 602 to Harborne Stephen? Officers' Ball in Burlington House, Glasgow, December 1950
Left to right: Hector McLean, H M Stephen, Dunlop Urie, Donald Jack, Archie Robinson and Marcus Robinson.

Group of ground-crew with Alex Bowman in front of Spitfire 21, LA319, LO-G, at Middle Wallop during Exercise 'Emperor', October 1950.

Spitfire F22; PK547, LO-J at RAF Middle Wallop as above.

Spitfire 22; PK395, LO-F at RAF Middle Wallop during Exercise 'Emperor', 7th to 15th October 1950. Alex Bowman about to fire-up, Bill Meldrum seems unimpressed.

One of the two silver Spitfire 22s, PK651 LO-N, at Renfrew during the summer of 1950. This was officially 602's last Spitfire.

The end of an era—Clydeside Spitfires replaced by jets.
For the Press, on Saturday 27th January 1951, one of 602's last remaining Spitfires, a Mk.22 (possibly PK349, LO-D) formates with one of the new Vampire jets along Renfrew's main runway (now the line of the M8 motorway).

After sustaining damage to undercarriage on take-off, Spitfire 21, LA329 overturned on landing at Renfrew on 4th May 1950. Pilot Frank Scott—unhurt.

602, with its new Vampire jets meets
the Press at Renfrew on Saturday 27th
January 1951.
Striding forward are, left to right,
Messrs. Paul Reid, Jack Laird, Johnny
McGuire (rear), Jack Daly, Jim
Johnston, Bill MacGregor, Alex
Bowman, Ian Hogg and Ian Paxton.

The two Meteor T7s supplied by Fighter
Command Scottish Sector HQ to give
the Press jet trips. VZ633, ZD-Z (222
Squadron) and WA729.

602, men and machines at Renfrew just prior to mobilisation, February 1951.

Flt Sgt Harry Henderson being presented with the BEM by Air Marshal Sir Basil Embry, C in C Fighter Command at RAF Leuchars, 1951.

602's pilots at Leuchars during the call-up in 1951.

Vampire FB5, WA315, LO-L at Renfrew with Alex Bowman in cockpit, November 1951. In the background are Sabres of the Royal Canadian Air Force on delivery to North Luffenham having been shipped to the nearby King George V Dock, transferred by road to Renfrew, prepared and flown-out—a common wartime use for Renfrew.

One of 602's Meteor T7 trainers, WF846, LO-V undergoing maintenance in one of the old (original) hangers at Renfrew.

Harvard KF920, LO-Z, beside 602's other Bessoneau hangar at the back of Renfrew.

RAF Leuchers, 1951 during mobilisation showing Scottish Auxiliary Wing.
602 with Vampires, 612 with Spitfire 16s and 603 with Spitfire 22s.

602's Pipe Band at Leuchars during mobilisation in May 1951.
Archie Robinson, Officer i/c is centre left and Pipe Major Iain MacLeod is centre right.

KF920, LO-Z, one of 602's Harvard trainers landing at Renfrew.

Meteor T7, WF773, LO-W at Renfrew.

With the River Clyde and its shipyards in the background, two Vampires make a formation take-off from Renfrew.

WA137, LO-D lands over what is now a bridge crossing the M8 Motorway. A Ford V8 Pilot awaits.

A cartoon by 'Roy' published in the 'Scottish Field'. May 1952.

F/LT BIRKIE BROWN   S/LDR H.M. STEPHEN D.S.O. D.F.C   P/O DON ELLIOT   F/O IAN PAXTON   F/O STAN HILSON   F/LT 'DOC' STEWART

F/LT BILL MacGREGGOR   (C.O.)   F/LT TOM WRIGHT   F/LT BOB ROBINSON   F/LT ALAN POWELL D.F.C.   F/LT JOHN BOND

F/O JACK FORREST   F/LT ARCHIE ROBINSON D.F.C   GLEN NIVEN

F/LT FREDDIE MORRIS

F/LT TOMMY BARRON

F/LT ROBIN REID

F/O JIMMY JOHNSTON D.F.C.

Roy 52

WE840, LO-L after a well-executed wheels-up landing at Renfrew on 6th September 1952, due to damage sustained after a mid-air collision during formation flying. The pilot, Ian Hogg was unhurt.

The Scottish Auxiliary Wing at RAF Turnhouse—Vampires of 602, 603 and 612 Squadrons.

One of the three Vampire F3s used by 602 for a short while in 1952. VF335 is seen in the winter snow at Renfrew bearing the code of a previous owner.

VV567, LO-K after flaming-out at Renfrew.

Line-up at Pembrey, July 1954 during annual camp.

VV567, now camouflaged, after over-shooting on landing at Abbotsinch in bad weather, 27th November 1954. pilot, Wilson Galloway unhurt.

The trail of VV567 on the 27th of November 1954

What might, indeed was intended to have been. The new equipment for the Fighter Squadrons of the Auxiliary Air Force, the Hawker Hunter. WT578 from the Central Fighter Establishment being demonstrated at Turnhouse to the Scottish Auxiliary Wing on 28/29th August 1954 by Sqn Ldr Seaton.

VZ345, 'L', now with its Grey Douglas markings lands at Abbotsinch, 1955.

The Grey Douglas markings on the Meteor T7, WF846 'V' landing at Abbotsinch. 1955?

Those who make it possible.

*Officers and their ladies at the Scottish
Auxiliary Wing Ball at Gleneagles,
October 1954.
In front are Messrs Gray, Mackay, Hogg
and Johnston.*

"For a fortnight, 125 Glasgow civilians are back in uniform again—and enjoying it! They are the 25 officers and 100 ground-crew of the famous 602 (City of Glasgow) Squadron of the Royal Auxiliary Air Force now attending their annual camp, this year at RAF Horsham St Faith, near Norwich in East Anglia."

Photo shows some of the Auxiliary Pilots of 602 Squadron being briefed by their CO, Squadron Leader R B Davidson, DFC. They are (l to r)—Fg Off I E Hogg, Fg Off K A McKay, Flt Lt J A Johnston DFC, Flt Lt R C Bridges, Fg Off W McNab, Fg Off J McGuire, Fg Off Gilbert and Flt Sgt J Watson.

Air Commodore Robinson (yet another!)
Fighter Command Caledonian Sector
Commander presents the trophies to
Messrs Bowman and Philip.
He is assisted by Sqn Ldr Davidson.
602's annual ball, January 1956.

Left to right: Messrs. Walker, Gray,
Winchester, Bartman (CO), Wilson,
Lockwood, Daly, MacGowan and Philip
decorate a Vampire.

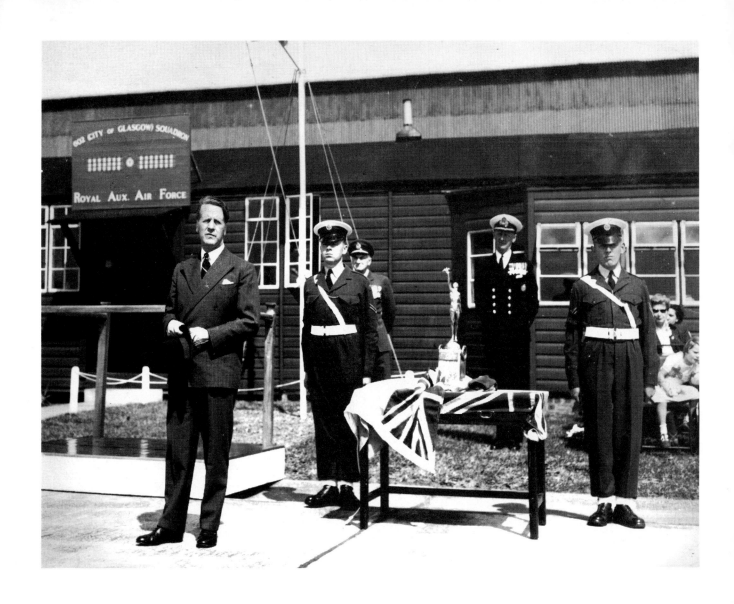

*The Duke of Hamilton prepares to pre-
sent the Cooper Trophy (for the Auxiliary Squadron making the greatest pro-
gress) to 602 on Saturday 23rd June
1956 at RNAS Abbotsinch.*

602's last annual camp at RAF North Front, Gibraltar on July 1956. Here, Vampire 5 WA196 'F' poses on the dispersal.

Not to be forgotten, a group of 602's regular airmen and NCO's.

Last 'Dining-in' night for 602 at their town HQ, Coplaw Street, Glasgow on Wednesday 23rd January 1957. Guest of Honour was Gp Capt Marcus Robinson deputising for the Duke of Hamilton. As the final entry in 602's Operations Record Book says "Good feelings not so good".

Vampire line-up at Abbotsinch 1956. Second aircraft from left is one of the FB9s, WR261 'C'.

Fg Off Peter Bell receives 602's Royal Standard from the Duke of Hamilton, Hon Air Commodore at Coplaw Street on Sunday 3rd March 1957. It was thereafter laid-up in Glasgow Cathedral.

Final parade.
Sqn Ldr Don Bartman and his men bid farewell! Abbotsinch, Sunday 27th January 1957.

1948

Ian Hogg and Jim Johnston.

1948

1940

Marcus Robinson, Donald Jack.

1940

Sandy Johnstone cutting 60th Anniversary cake!
Bill McConnell, the man behind the 602 Museum, looks on.

60th anniversary celebrations at the 602 Museum, Hillington, September 1985 . . . and as they were forty or so years ago.

1940

1940

Glen Niven talks to Mr and Mrs Dunlop Urie.

1940

TB308, a Spitfire LF XVIe, acting as a
gate guardian at RAF Bishopbriggs near
Glasgow. She was given to 602 for
instructional duties in 1954 and
was orignally intended to be mounted
outside the new terminal at Renfrew.

Spitfire Ia, R6915 which flew with 602
at Prestwick during 1941.
It is preserved in the Imperial War
Musem at Lambeth.

Bill McConnell and cadets in the 602 Museum which they devised and built.

Outside the new 602 Museum at Hillington, brought about by the initiative of 2175 (Rolls Royce) Squadron Air Training Corps, stands one of the RAF Exhibition Flight's Spitfire 16s. TB382 flew with 602 in 1945 and it was fitting that she guarded the Museum on the occasion of its opening by Marshal of the Royal Air Force Lord Cameron of Balhousie on Saturday 22nd October 1983.

On 6th June 1986, nearly forty years after she served with 602, Spitfire F21, LA198, RAI-G is dedicated as gate guardian at RAF Leuchars. She flew with 602 between 1947 and 1949 and almost certainly operated from Leuchars. Many of those who flew her were present on the day.

Vampire F3, VT812 which flew with 602 during 1952 and 1953.
It is preserved in the RAF Museum Hendon in the markings of 601 Squadron with which it also flew.

34089, "602 Squadron", a 'Battle of Britain' class 4-6-2 locomotive, built in December 1948. Rebuilt by British Railways, it was withdrawn in July 1967.

Nameplate from 34089

After the outbreak of war, 602 maintained its connections with the City of Glasgow. The Lord Provost of the time, 'Paddy' (later Sir Patrick), Dollan took great pride in the City's Fighter Squadron—'Pat's Own' as he liked to call them. With Sandy Johnstone, CO at the time he founded a Trust Fund during 1940 to help members of the Squadron in time of need and with a view to assisting resettlement after the war. Paddy Dollan was a great wartime Lord Provost and a powerful figure in the West of Scotland.

An early beneficiary of the fund was the son of Norman Stone, one of the pre-war pilots, who was killed in a flying accident during the war. The fund helped to educate him at Glasgow Academy. He later became Professor of Modern History at the University of Oxford.

During 1986 the Fund was wound-up for all practical purposes with the remaining monies being disbursed to various Service charities including Erskine Hospital.

Group Captain George Pinkerton presenting a cheque for £465.00 to Erskine Hospital, for disabled ex-servicemen, on Wednesday 25th March 1987.
The money was raised from the sale of the prints of a painting by Dugald Cameron of the action over the Firth of Forth on 16th October 1939, when George Pinkerton shot down the first enemy aircraft over the UK of the Second World War.

George Pinkerton on the 47th anniversary of his shooting-down of the first enemy aircraft over the U.K.
Flying with the West of Scotland Flying Club at Abbotsinch on 16th October 1986.

Year 1950		AIRCRAFT		Pilot, or 1st Pilot	2nd Pilot, Pupil or Passenger	DUTY (Including Results and Remarks)
Month	Date	Type	No.			
—	—	—	—	—	—	Totals Brought Forward
Oct.	1	HARVARD.	LO.Y.	SELF.	P.11 DALY.	FORMATION
"	1	"	LO.X.	"	P.11 REID.	MUTUAL 18.
"	7	SPITFIRE	LOY.	"	—	RENFREW TO LINTON ON OUSE.
"	7	"	LOY	"	—	LINTON TO MIDDLE WALLOP.
"	12	"	LOY	"	—	AIRTEST Q.G.H.
"	12	"	LO.F.	"	—	AIRTEST.
"	14	"	LO.F.	"	—	EXERCISE EMPEROR.
"	15	"	'A'	"	—	MIDDLE WALL. TO RENFREW.
"	28	"	LOY	"	—	CINÉ GUN.
"	28	"	630.	"	—	CINÉ GUN.
		Summary for Oct. '50			1. SPITFIRE	
		Unit : 602. Squadron.			2. HARVARD.	
		Date :- 1st Nov. 50				
		Signature : Alt Bowman				
Nov.	4	SPITFIRE	LOY.	SE		
"	5	"	LO.A			
"	5	HARVARD.	LOX			
"	11	SPITFIRE	LO.O.			
"	11	HARVARD	LO.X.			
"	13	SPITFIRE	LO.O.			
"	13	"	LO.O.			
"	26	HARVARD.	LO.X.			

| YEAR 1954 | | AIRCRAFT | | PILOT, OR | 2ND PILOT, PUPIL | DUTY |
MONTH	DATE	Type	No.	1ST PILOT	OR PASSENGER	(INCLUDING RESULTS AND REMARKS)
—	—	—	—	—	—	TOTALS BROUGHT FORWARD
JULY	18	VAMPIRE	E	SELF		TO PEMBREY
"	18	VAMPIRE	L	SELF		SECTOR RECCE
"	18	VAMPIRE	D	SELF		¼ ATTACKS
"	18	VAMPIRE	E	SELF		FORMATION
"	19	VAMPIRE	B	SELF		AIR TO AIR FIRING
"	19	VAMPIRE	E	SELF		AIR TO AIR FIRING
"	19	VAMPIRE	E	SELF		AIR TO AIR FIRING
"	21	VAMPIRE	G	SELF		AIR TO AIR FIRING
"	21	VAMPIRE	B	SELF		AIR TO AIR FIRING
"	22	VAMPIRE	A	SELF		AIR TO AIR FIRING
"	22	VAMPIRE	L	SELF		AIR TO AIR FIRING
"	22	VAMPIRE	B	SELF		AIR TO AIR FIRING.
						AIR TO AIR FIRING.

GRAND TOTAL [Cols. (1) to (10)]
1870 Hrs. 55 Mins.   TOTALS CARRIED FORWARD

143

Former members of 602 with David Roberts, Managing Director of Glasgow Airport, after the unveiling of a sculpture by Eric Kennington ARA, at Glasgow Airport, Abbotsinch on Wednesday 24th June 1987. The symbolic piece, entitled "1940 Group" was exhibited at the exhibition of the Royal Glasgow Institute of the Fine Arts in the Autumn of 1954. It was purchased by subscription by members of the Glasgow Art Club and two anonymous donors in memory of 602 City of Glasgow Squadron, Royal Auxiliary Air Force.

HOME DEFENCE 1940-1945

BATTLE OF BRITAIN 1940

FORTRESS EUROPE 1940-1944

CHANNEL AND NORTH SEA 1940-1943

DIEPPE

FRANCE AND GERMANY 1944-1945

CAVE LEONEM CRUCIATUM

NORMANDY 1944

*"It is an ancient and laudable custom to lay up in the House of God
the consecrated emblems of man's duty and service,
there to remain for all times as a reminder of duty well done
and of the strength that God supplies."*

I

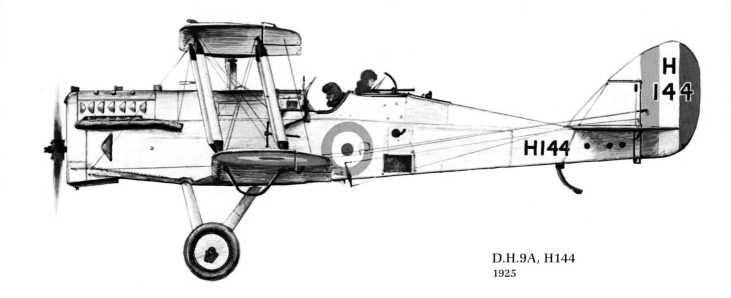

D.H.9A, H144
1925

Hart, K3865, 'B' Flight
1936

Hawker Hind over Tait's Tower,
Empire Exhibition, Bellahouston Park,
Glasgow, October 1938.

Flt Lt George Pinkerton attacking and downing a Ju88 of KG30 over the Firth of Forth near Crail on the afternoon of the 16th October 1939. This was during the first conclusive Fighter Command action of the War for which Pinkerton was awarded the DFC. He shared the attack with Archie McKellar.

Spitfire Ia, L1004 'LO-Q'
1940

Spitfire L.F. XVIe, TB382 'LO-Z'
1945

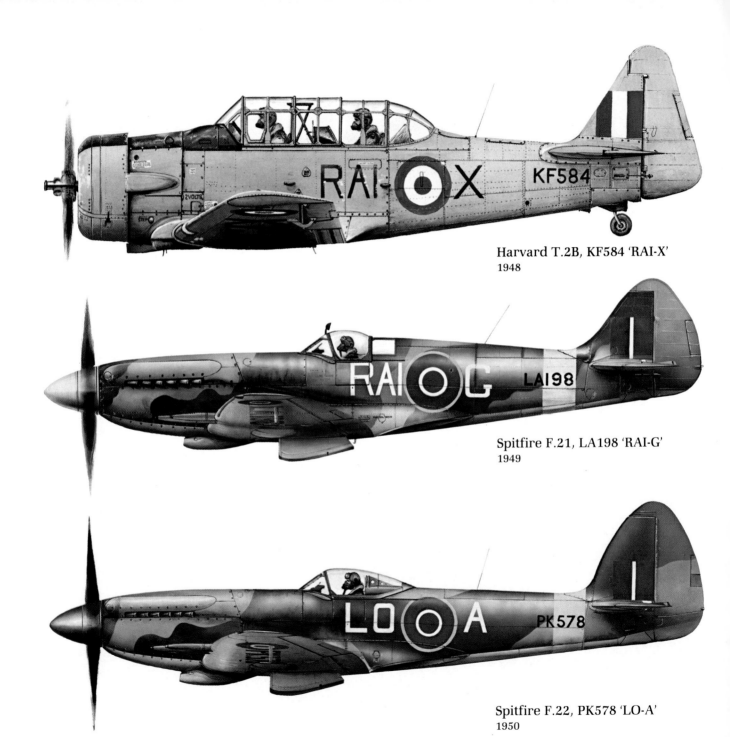

Harvard T.2B, KF584 'RAI-X'
1948

Spitfire F.21, LA198 'RAI-G'
1949

Spitfire F.22, PK578 'LO-A'
1950

Vampire FB.5, WA137 'LO-D'
1952

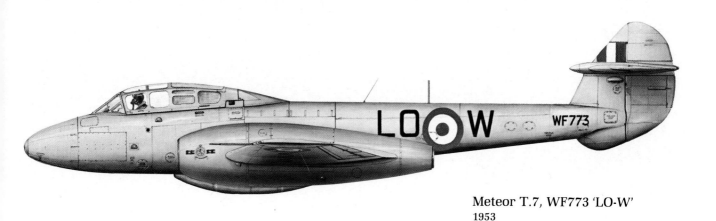

Meteor T.7, WF773 'LO-W'
1953

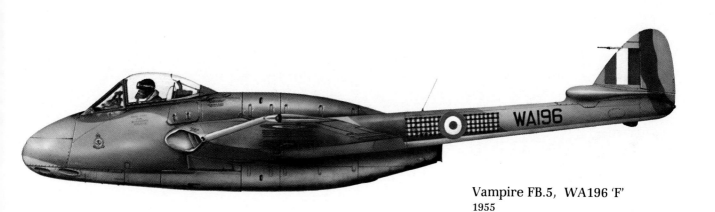

Vampire FB.5, WA196 'F'
1955

Vampire FB.5 over the Clyde, 1953.

APPENDICES

Abbreviations used in text

aban	*abandoned*	inj	*injured*
acc	*accident*	kld	*killed*
act	*action*	ldg	*landed/ing*
alloc	*allocated*	Mk	*mark*
allot	*alloted/ment*	mks	*marks/ings*
app	*approach*	nr	*near*
AuxAF	*Auxiliary Air Force*	ops	*operations*
ber	*beyond economic repair*	o/s	*overshot*
cd	*crashed*	o/t	*overturned*
coll	*collided/sion*	Plt Off	*Pilot Officer*
conv	*converted*	PoW	*Prisoner of War*
cr/ld	*crash landed*	rep	*repaired/s*
dam	*damaged*	rtd	*returned*
dbf	*damaged by fire*	Sgt	*Sergeant*
dbr	*damaged beyond repair*	SOC	*struck off charge*
del	*delivery/ed*	Sqn Ldr	*Squadron Leader*
des	*destroyed*	s/dn	*shot down*
dev	*development*	s/up	*shot up*
e/an	*enemy action*	strk	*struck*
ea/a	*enemy aircraft*	trg	*training*
fce/ld	*force landed/ing*	t/o	*take off*
fin	*finished*	u/c	*undercarriage*
Flt Lt	*Flight Lieutenant*	Wg Cdr	*Wing Commander*
Fg Off	*Flying Officer*	WO	*Warrant Officer*
FTR	*failed to return*	w/o	*written off*
Gp Capt	*Group Captain*	w/u	*wheels up*
grd	*ground*	WFU	*withdrawn from use*

APPENDIX I

The Men of 602 (City of Glasgow) Squadron
Honorary Air Commodores
Lord Stonehaven (Pre-War)
Duke of Hamilton and Brandon PC GCVO AFC DL (Post War)

Commanding Officers

Sqn Ldr C N Lowe MC DFC
(Sept 1925-Jan 1926)

Regular RAF Officer, appointed initially until first Auxiliary CO was available.

Capt J D Latta MC
(February 1926-May 1927)

First Auxiliary CO. Scout pilot in RFC during World War I.

Sqn Ldr J Fullerton
(May 1927-May 1932)

Served in Royal Engineers

The Marquess of Douglas and Clydesdale AFC, later His Grace, the 14th Duke of Hamilton and Brandon.
(May 1932-Sept 1936)

Scotland's premier Peer. One of the original members of 602. First man to fly over Mt. Everest (with Flt Lt D F McIntyre) on 3rd April 1933.

Sqn Ldr D F MacIntyre AFC
(Sept 1936-October 1937)

Responsible for the planning and development of Scottish Aviation Ltd and Prestwick Airport together with the then Marquess of Douglas and Clydesdale.

Sqn Ldr A D Farquhar DFC
(October 1937-April 1940)

Commanding Officer at the outbreak of war.

Sqn Ldr G C Pinkerton OBE DFC
(April 1940-July 1940)

As 'B' Flight commander, shot down a Ju88 during the first Fighter Command action of World War II, 16th October 1939.

Sqn Ldr A V R (Sandy) Johnstone DFC
(July 1940-April 1941)

CO during Battle of Britain
Retired from RAF in 1968 in the post of AOC Scotland and Northern Ireland

Sqn Ldr J I Kilmartin OBE DFC
(April 1941-June 1941)

Sqn Ldr P Meagher DSO DFC
(June 1941-August 1941)

Sqn Ldr A C (Al) Deere DSO OBE DFC
(August 1941-January 1942)

Sqn Ldr B (Paddy) Finucane DSO DFC
(January 1942-June 1942)

Killed in Action, 1944

Sqn Ldr P M Brothers DSO DFC
(June 1942-October 1942)

Sqn Ldr M F Beytagh DFC
(October 1942-October 1943)

Sqn Ldr R A (Max) Sutherland DFC
(October 1943-July 1944)

Sqn Ldr J J (Chris) Le Roux DFC   Killed in Action, 1944
(July 1944-August 1944)

Sqn Ldr R A (Max) Sutherland DFC
(August 1944-May 1945)

Flt Lt A R Stewart
(Temporarily August (1944)

Sqn Ldr Marcus Robinson AFC   Re-formed 602 as an Auxiliary Squadron
(September 1946-August 1950)   in 1946 having first joined 602 in 1934.

Sqn Ldr H M Stephen DSO DFC
(September 1950-July 1952)

Sqn Ldr J A (Jack) Forrest   Joined 602 as an NCO pilot in 1947. Last
(July 1952-October 1953)   Auxiliary CO

Sqn Ldr R B (Bert) Davidson DFC   Regular RAF Officer
(October 1953-May 1956)

Sqn Ldr C D (Don) Bartman   Regular RAF Officer. Disbanded 602 on
(May 1956-March 1957)   10th March 1957

Officers

Service No.		Date of Joining	Service No.		Date of Enlistment	Service No.		Date of Enlistment
	Lowe C N, MC DFC(RAF) *(1st CO, Regular Officer)*	14/9/25		Back, D H	/29	90163	Johnstone A V R	1/35
	Latta J D, MC	28/1/26		Ogilvie B C H	12/29		Hawkes J P	1/35
90173	Allan J C H	4/26		Lennox J S		90164	Urie J D	3/35
	Drew J P	4/26		Land	4/30	90169	Muspratt-Williams R J	
	Parker, C A S	7/26		Phillips	5/30	90165	Boyd R F	
	Davidson H G	7/26		Smith T B	6/30	90170	Jack D M	9/36
	McIntyre D F	3/27		Buchanan J O	10/30	90168	McKellar A A	9/36
90176	Marquess of Douglas & Clydesdale *(later 14th Duke of Hamilton & Brandon-1941)*	5/27	90179	Hodge J H	11/30	90166	McLean C H	
	Fullerton J	6/5/27	90178	Rintoul A	4/31	90171	Webb P C	
	Faulds R	7/27	70888	Law D W	6/31	90167	Ferguson P J	
	Horsburgh J K	10/27	90174	Sutherland L A, MA *(Chaplain until 1953)*	6/31	90172	Stone N	
90158	Farquhar A D	7/27		Renshaw C M B	10/31		Johnstone A E	5/38
	Falls	14/3/28	36027	Howell E A	2/32	90254	Graeme N S	
	Feather J S	/29	90181	Grant A M	6/32	90175	Richards R T	/39
	Stewart J R	/29		Kennedy K E	9/32	91226	Niven H G	2/39
	Murray F G	5/29		Ross	9/32		Gower R D	4/39
	Lloyd D L	5/29	90161	Robinson M	7/33			
	Mitchell W H	/29	90160	Pinkerton G C	10/33			
	McNab A D	/29	90162	Bell E V N	12/33			
				Shewell J M	7/34			

In April 1939, R F Phillips of 602 became the first aircraftsman to be accepted for pilot training, and subsequently commissioned. At about the outbreak of War 602 welcomed

Sergeants A (Pat) Lyall and H (Harry) W Moody, who were subsequently commissioned and both, sadly, lost their lives. Also, Flt Lt C J (Micky) Mount and Pilot Officers H C (Roger) Coverley and T G F Ritchie, 'Glyn' Ritchie the latter two were also to lose their lives.

Men

Service No.		Date of Enlistment
		1925
802000	McLaren A	8/12
001	Melville R	,,
002	Lenehan D J	,,
003	Dougall H	,,
004	McMaster D D	,,
005	Lawson W B	,,
006	McMaster A S	,,
007	Linn W	16/12
008	Macrae C J	,,
009	Gibb W	,,
010	Barrie T	,,
011	Findlay J C McL	,,
012	Wilson D	,,
014	Bruce H H	,,
015	Smillie T	,,
017	Deans A	,,
018	McTurk	,,
019	Dow D M	17/12
020	Rankine R	,,
021	Brown J H	,,
023	Moore T J A	,,
024	Cunningham H G	,,
026	Calder W	,,
027	Hobson G	,,
028	Harper J R	,,
029	Baird H S	,,
030	Monie R	,,
031	Strain J	,,
032	Renfrew A W	,,
033	Gray A	,,
022	Dunn J	18/12
025	McMurtrie H C	,,

Service No.		Date of Enlistment
034	Beveridge J C	18/12
035	Harper T	,,
036	Kinnear R	,,
037	McAlliaster R	,,
038	Mckay E F	,,
039	McPherson W	,,
040	Stevenson P McP	,,
041	Downie A W	,,
043	Kirkwood A S	,,
044	Eadie R G	,,
045	White W	,,
046	Ferguson W	,,
047	Wilson W J	,,
048	Wood J	,,
013	Wylie D B	17/12
052	Walker J M	18/12
		1926
049	McCall D	5/1
050	Gunn P J	,,
051	Bowie C	,,
053	McEachern D J	,,
054	McLeod A	,,
056	Coulter A G	,,
057	Coubrough J	,,
058	MacDonald C H	,,
059	McCartney S M	,,
060	Kane J B	,,
042	Kettle E S	7/1
055	Hossack A	,,
061	Mickie A S	,,
062	Smith J M	,,
063	Watson A C	,,
064	McQuarrie R F	,,
065	Malcolm R	,,
066	Russell A B	,,
067	Weir A	,,
068	Bell T	6/2
069	McKechnie W	12/1
070	Pailthorpe G	,,
071	Scott J R	,,
072	Stewart C	,,
073	Russell J	,,
074	Nairn J D	9/2

Service No.		Date of Enlistment
075	Davis S F	12/1
076	Ryburn J F	,,
077	Adams F G	27/3
078	Clarke H M	,,
079	Morrison J A	,,
080	Young W	,,
081	Reid A McL	,,
082	Rodger J	,,
083	Irving R	24/4
084	Harvie W	15/6
085	Murray T	,,
086	Warnock J M	,,
087	Park W J	,,
088	Nairn G A	,,
089	Martin A L	,,
090	Lees J S	,,
091	Nisbet T McP	19/6
092	Hanratty W	19/10
093	Sinclair J	,,
094	Bain E J W	7/12
		1927
095	Devine	23/2
096	Brown J A	22/3
097	Phillips R S	5/4
098	Miller R F	,,
099	Hossack J M B	17/4
100	Kerr G S	,,
101	Robertson W T B	26/4
102	Douglas J B	,,
103	Fraser A	30/5
104	Addison G	5/6
105	Dowson J	,,
106	McNidder A B	9/6
107	Ball J D	4/7
108	MacAllister F F	15/8
109	McBryer W J	,,
110	MacIntyre D	,,
111	Crawford J	,,
112	Meechan H	1/9
113	McMillan W	,,
114	Kinnell S D	14/9
115	Alexander P	28/9

Service No.		Date of Enlistment	Service No.		Date of Enlistment	Service No.		Date of Enlistment
116	Waters A G	,,	158	McPherson G	,,	200	Bennett J	,,
117	Fraser W J	,,	159	Mathieson A W	,,	201	McIntyre J B A	,,
118	Park A	13/10	160	Miller R	,,	202	Kearney M	,,
119	Kettle J	19/10	161	Stevenson A P	,,	203	Stoddart D R	15/6
120	Hay R R	,,	162	Grier W	,,	204	McLachlan J B	,,
121	Garman L	25/10	163	Liddell J	,,	205	Loche J S P	,,
122	Steel T	2/11	164	Macdonald A	,,	206	Findlayson L D P A	,,
123	Gilliland J	16/11	165	Goodwin C	,,	207	Holmes R J	,,
124	Howe R K	7/12	166	Stark D F	,,	208	Reid D	,,
		1928	167	Geary P C	,,	209	Hamilton T H M	,,
125	Scott	20/2	168	Sangster G B	,,	210	Pattison R R	29/6
126	McPhee J	,,	169	McMaster T B	,,	211	Garden R L	9/10
127	Wilson J J	27/2	170	Parker H A	,,	212	Wilson J	,,
128	Alcorn I	,,	171	Hunter J	,,	213	Watt J	,,
129	Steele J	,,	172	Campbell D H C	,,	214	Scott R	28/10
130	Clark R B	,,	173	Mason W	,,	215	Russell A A	6/11
131	Connell P W	,,	174	Campbell A W S	,,	216	Magee R B	,,
132	Davidson M	5/3	175	Robertson J	,,	217	Smith C	,,
133	MacGibbon C G	19/3	176	Breen J	,,	218	Russell A	,,
134	Tait G R	21/3	177	Montgomery J A	,,	219	Bradley J M	,,
135	Barclay R A	4/4	178	Brwon J F	,,	220	McLaughlan J H	,,
136	Doig R	11/4	179	Clarke J C	26/9	221	Simcox T	,,
137	Kerr A	,,	180	Wilson R	15/10	222	McMillan A R M	20/11
138	Bain A T	,,	181	McFarlane J M	26/10	223	McNaught S	27/11
139	Anderson J	2/5	182	Macintyre H E	7/12	224	Tinto P L	,,
140	Mabberly P	,,	183	Forrest W J McM	22/12			1930
141	Miller R	,,	184	Haggerty R	,,	225	Fraser D	8/1
142	Boyd D	9/5			1929	226	Cook J H	,,
143	Muir J	23/5	185	Graham G B	7/1	227	Martin J A M	,,
144	Blair J	2/6	186	McFarlane C D	21/1	228	Miller W A	,,
145	Barron R B	3/6	187	Clay J	,,	229	Davidson W	,,
146	Sherry J J	2/6	188	Wilkinson W A	11/2	230	Morton J	,,
147	Ford J	4/6	189	Smith E E	13/3	231	McGregor J P	,,
148	Faulds J S	10/6	190	Leckie H K	10/4	232	Ballantine A M	,,
149	Faulds J S	,,	191	Halfpenny F A	1/5	233	Murphy J B	29/1
150	McAllister A	2/7	192	Herring A	,,	234	McAllister H W	,,
151	McChesney J	5/9	193	Paton R	21/5	235	Wilson G	,,
152	Barriskell R	,,	194	Gordon R	,,	236	Arthur T	26/2
153	Blair G	,,	195	Davies J F	1/6	237	Sowter G R	12/3
154	Begg A S	,,	196	Rutherford J	,,	238	Money W	24/3
155	Fordyce A	,,	197	Muir W C	,,	239	Dawson A C	,,
156	Hanley D M	,,	198	Inglis R W	,,	240	Money R	,,
157	Tarbert J	,,	199	MacDonald A J	,,	241	Whyte W B	9/4

Service No.		Date of Enlistment	Service No.		Date of Enlistment	Service No.		Date of Enlistment
242	Brownlie A	30/4	285	Gordon L R	4/6	325	Hutton D S	16/3
243	Binnie J	1/6	286	Balneaves R	,,	326	Riley A T	,,
244	Brown J S F	12/6	287	Hughes C H	25/6	327	Hunter W E	,,
245	Lindsay W S	22/6	288	McMaster C C	,,	328	Gordon J	22/4
246	McAllister I A J	,,	289	Carstairs E B M	,,	329	Gray A	,,
247	Brown W H	,,	290	Brady J	10/9	330	Millar W	,,
248	McFadyen J	,,	291	Henderson H J	,,	331	McDonald T G	14/5
249	McGuigan W H	,,	292	Macfarlane S	27/9	332	Carswell D	,,
250	Brown N	,,	293	Mackenzie T K M	5/11	333	Paton J R	,,
252	Bradley W W	,,	294	McCall W	,,	334	Knox G S B	,,
253	Hartley J	6/7	295	Bell B	,,	335	Maxwell S B M	,,
254	Stoddart A R	5/10	296	Hamilton J M	22/11	336	McLean J	28/5
255	Wilson J A	,,	297	Young J R D W	,,	337	Clark A B	8/10
256	Leonard P M	30/10	298	Inglis M R	3/12	338	Calgie J	,,
257	Ingram W	13/11	299	Dobbin W	10/12	339	Erwin J	,,
258	Gray J C	16/11	300	Downie E	,,	340	Harrison J	,,
259	Brown G	,,	301	Young T W	,,	341	Hamilton W	,,
260	Burns J J	27/11				342	Perry T A	,,
261	Montgomery W B	18/12			**1932**	343	Burnside A	,,
262	Barbour W A G	,,	302	Wilson W D	21/1	344	Maclachlan N D	15/10
		1931	303	Jack R W H	14/2	345	Garside H	,,
263	McNeish W	5/1	304	McMurtrie J	8/4	346	Blair H	,,
264	Shaw W	,,	305	Coggleg A W	12/4	347	Mackay G A F	26/10
265	Gray W	,,	306	Franks G	,,	348	Eltringham J	,,
266	McLester D N	12/1	307	Rutherford A H	,,	349	Gibb W K	,,
267	Hyland M	,,	308	McIntosh A C R	,,	350	Crawford T	12/11
268	Sweet W H S	22/1	309	Falconer J	15/4	351	Kennedy J L	,,
269	Jolly H R	29/1	310	Humphrey J S	,,	352	Thomson G	
270	Miller O	8/3	311	Gibb G J	,,	353	Johnstone A G	
271	Sloan W	,,	312	Cranston A S	,,	354	Hamilton A M	
272	Rae G	,,	313	Wilson J	,,	355	Welsh G C	
273	James G G	,,	314	Kay H	24/4	356	Nelson F T	
274	Carrigan S	,,	315	Sinclair P M	6/5	357	McMillan J	
275	Lapham E Y	,,	316	Wilson W H	,,	358	Hair J	
276	Marshall T	19/3	317	Johnstone J C	12/6	359	Aitken W	
277	Strain J	26/4	318	Pfeiffer C A	12/10	360	Logan J	
278	Wilson T C	,,	319	Macpherson N C	,,	361	Armstrong W J	
279	Beaumont J W	10/5	320	Seivwright W	30/10	362	Mitchell N	
280	Moonie J	30/5	321	Steel R	,,	363	Falconer N A	
281	Brownlie A M S	,,	322	Weir J	20/11	364	McColl H	
282	Methven R A	,,			**1933**	365	Currie W J	
283	Creelman S	,,	323	Kay W	12/1	366	Allison W S	
284	McNair A A	,,	324	Kerr A S	26/2	367	McGregor T S	

Service No.		Date of Joining	Service No.		Date of Joining	Service No.		Date of Enlistment
368	Hornsby R J		408	Brown W M	,,	450	Macgregor A	,,
369	More C		409	McIntosh C L	,,	451	Boyd G S	,,
370	Morris D H		410	Briggs L	,,	452	McKinnon W M	,,
371	Anderson A		411	Douglas W	,,	453	Scott G	,,
372	McLachlan J		412	Robb W	,,	454	Macrea H S	,,
373	Lennon F		413	Creelman A	3/3	455	McCracken L	1/3
		1933	414	Urquhart W	,,	456	Stevenson R M	15/3
374	McEwan O		415	Brown J	,,	457	Lochhead J	26/4
375	Irvine G L		416	Paton R R A	,,	458	McRobert C	,,
376	Cunningham P		417	Kirkpatrick A	,,	459	Simpson G	17/5
377	Morrison N		418	Cairnduff A	17/3	460	McTaggart J A	,,
378	Perfect W		419	Jeffrey A	,,	461	McIntyre G R	,,
379	Brown A M		420	Stewart S L	18/4	462	Lauder A	,,
380	Conway G		421	McGinnes E	,,	463	Crossan J M	,,
381	Cowie W		422	Ferguson J	28/4	464	Hamilton W J	24/5
382	Walls F		423	Malcolm T	,,	465	Herring L E	,,
383	Scott T		424	Houston J	1/6	466	Tasker J A	,,
384	Skimming D M		425	Ness M	8/6	467	Davidson C H	8/6
385	Forsyth J		426	Bryson J	,,	468	Murray W B	,,
386	Hall W L		427	Moore G	,,	469	Oliver W B	1/11
387	Finnie D		428	Clark R	,,	470	Harper E	,,
388	Roxburgh A J		429	Thomson J	,,	471	Burnett R G	,,
389	Hamilton A M		430	Bain A	,,	472	Day L J	,,
390	McFarlane A		431	Bennett M	,,	473	Cooper R G	,,
391	Carey J D		432	Davidson G	22/9	474	Buchanan D	,,
392	Graham J		433	Cowan W H	,,	475	Clark J	15/11
393	Lewis J		434	McAlpine W	29/9	476	Gordon A M	,,
394	Keppie E D F		435	McLeod A	3/11	477	Brownlie W	,,
395	Miller J		436	Collins N W	,,	478	Anderson J	,,
396	Dickson J J		437	Young S	,,	479	Steele G	29/11
397	Maxwell R F		438	Bell G	,,	480	Pearson R S	6/12
398	Brodie W C		439	Nicol W P	,,	481	Wherry F L	,,
399	Burnhill J		440	Dawson W G	,,	482	Gibson J S	,,
400	Hutton J		441	MacDonald H A	24/11	483	Reid A	,,
401	Waddell T J, DFM		442	Primrose J	,,	484	Douglas H A	
402	Vance J M		443	Elliott J R	,,			
			444	Brown M	,,			1937
		1935			1936	486	Paterson N A	17/1
403	Fairweather W D	27/1	445	Duncan T	12/1	487	Rae J	
404	Sparks E	,,	446	Parnie J A	,,	488	Deans J C	
405	Keane W	,,	447	Martin W B	,,	489	Brownlee W A	
406	McLaren W	3/2	448	Bryce H H	,,	490	Third H	
407	Colquhoun J	,,	449	Outch T G	,,	491	Graham J W	

Service No.	Name	Date of Joining	Service No.	Name	Date of Joining	Service No.	Name	Date of Enlistment
492	Robb E		534	Hastie W K	,,	575	Douglas D W	12/3
493	Woodward J D		535	Leighton J	,,	576	Smith M A	,,
494	Mooney J		536	Sands V	,,	577	McLauchlan J S	,,
495	Pope J		537	Walker J A	3/2	578	Martin J	,,
496	Aitken G S		538	Pollock G	,,	579	Westwood C C	,,
497	Crooks A J		539	Thompson W B	11/2	580	Jones N	,,
498	Murray C		540	Macbride W	5/3	581	Hannah H	,,
499	Wood J L		541	Davie E	,,	582	Mackay A	,,
500	Gilmour T		542	Rankine A	,,	583	Parker J	,,
501	Montgomery C		543	Cockburn H	,,	584	Leslie M	,,
502	Kennedy W R		544	Sayers C	,,	585	Yuill M M	,,
503	Hempkin J K		545	Stevenson T R	24/3	586	Blackie W	26/3
504	Malcolm J		546	Lowe F	,,	587	Shaw J M	,,
505	Steele B		547	Low K	,,	588	Hicks W	20/4
506	Phillips R F	5/6	548	Chisholm D	,,	589	Eveleigh S	,,
507	Henry J		549	Brown W	,,	590	Jones R	,,
508	Macdonald A H		550	Herd J	,,	591	Rae J A	,,
509	Lamont A		551	Horne I	,,	592	Thomas D L	,,
510	Sharp R		552	Richardson T	21/4	593	McIntyre T V K	,,
511	Wallace A G		553	Mitchell A	,,	594	Davis A F	,,
512	Richard P	24/10	554	Leslie J	,,	595	Hutchinson S A	20/4
513	McGonigle J	,,	555	Maguire A	,,	596	Davis J M F	7/5
514	Cooper D D	,,	556	Anderson J	,,	597	Clark A J	14/5
515	Finch G	,,	557	Noble J	,,	598	Wilson A R	4/6
516	Flower W O	,,	558	Young J B	,,	599	Bryden J H	,,
517	Manston J M	25/11	559	Brown R	,,			
518	Young E A	,,	560	Rankin G	21/4			1939
519	Dewar C D W	,,	561	McBride A F	2/6	740540600	Bryden J M	
520	Heavisides W L	,,	562	Hay E A	1/10		Killed 9/39 in night flying accident.	
521	Nelson J M	,,					(Transfer from RAFVR)	9/6
522	McCairns G	,,			1939	740540601	McAdam D W	
523	Livingston M	5/12	563	Muir M	29/1		(Transfer from RAFVR)	9/6
524	Pomphrey D	,,	564	Reid A W	,,	740540602	McDowall A	
525	Brocket J	,,	565	Wherry H W	,,		(Transfer from RAFVR)	9/6
		1938	566	Kerr W A	,,			
526	Reid S M D	27/1	567	McArthur J M	,,			1936
527	Rendall D	,,	568	Rae G	,,	803181	Young R B	20/1
528	Mood J	,,	569	Robb H M P	,,		(Transfer from 603 Sqn)	
529	Moore S	,,	570	Arnott T	,,			
530	McKinnon G	,,	571	Campbell I K	,,			
531	Gordon A	,,	572	Shaw A	,,			
532	Murdoch A S	,,	573	Rice E	,,			
533	Outch G	,,	574	Coventry J D	13/2			

Officers and aircrew at the outbreak of War
3rd September 1939

Commanding Officer	Squadron Leader	A D Farquhar
OC 'A' Flight	Flight Lieutenant	M Robinson
OC 'B' Flight	Flight Lieutenant	G C Pinkerton
	Flight Lieutenant	J Hozier Hodge (AAF Reserve)
	Flight Lieutenant	E V N Bell (Aux Adjutant)
	Flight Lieutenant	A V R Johnstone
	Flight Lieutenant	J Dunlop Urie
	Flying Officer	A M Grant (AAF Reserve)
	Flying Officer	R F Boyd
	Flying Officer	C Hector MacLean
	Flying Officer	P J 'Ian' Ferguson
	Flying Officer	Archie A McKellar
	Flying Officer	Donald M Jack
	Flying Officer	R Muspratt-Williams
	Flying Officer	Paul E Webb
	Flying Officer	Norman Stonc
	Pilot Officer	N Graeme
	Pilot Officer	H G Niven
	Sergeant	Andrew McDowall
	Sergeant	J M Bryden (subsequently killed night-flying at Abbotsinch)
	Sergeant	D W Macadam
	Sergeant	R F Philips
Medical Officer	Squadron Leader	J C W Allan
Padre		Rev Lewis A Sutherland (Minister of the Church of the Holy Rude Stirling)
Accountant Officer	Flight Lieutenant	Andrew Rintoul (pre-war pilot)

Additional strength was soon added by:—

	Sergeant	A 'Pat' Lyall
	Sergeant	H W Moody
	Pilot Officer	Hugh 'Roger' Coverley
	Flight Lieutenant	C J Mount
	Pilot Officer	T Glyn Ritchie

Information taken from a letter to the Lord Provost of Glasgow by the father of Fg Off Hector MacLean, 24 January 1941.

602 Squadron, Jan. 1940

S/Ldr A D Farquhar Commanding Officer
F/Lt M Robinson 'A' Flight Commander
F/Lt A V R Johnstone 'B' Flight Commander

'A' Flt, commanded by F/Lt J D Urie from 25/4/40 on Marcus Robinson's promotion to command 616 Squadron

Squadron pilots during the 'Battle of Britain' (July—Sept 15th 1940)

Plt Off E W Aries
Sgt C F Babbage
Fg Off P C C Barthropp
Flt Lt R F Boyd ('B' Flight Commander)
Sgt Bracton
Fg Off W H Coverley (Killed in action*)
Sgt A W Eade
Plt Off A L Edy (Killed in action)
Sgt D W Elcombe (Killed in action*)
Fg Off P J Ferguson
Plt Off G Fisher
Plt Off D H Gage (Killed in action)
Flt Sgt J Gillies (Killed in action)
Plt Off O V Hanbury (Killed in action)
Fg Off J S Hart
Plt Off W P Hopkin
Plt Off D M Jack
Sq Ldr A V R Johnstone
    (CO during 'Battle of Britain')
Plt Off A Lyall (Killed in action)
Fg Off C H MacLean
Sgt A McDowall
Plt Off H W Moody (Killed in action*)
Fg Off C J Mount
    ('A' Flight Commander after Dunlop Urie)
Plt Off H G Niven
Plt Off R A Payne (Killed in action)

Sgt J Proctor
Plt Off T G F Ritchie
Plt Off S N Rose
Sgt W B Smith
Sgt M H Sprague (Killed in action*)
Flt Lt J D Urie ('A' Flight Commander)
Fg Off P C Webb
Sgt B E P Whall (Killed in action*)
Sgt G A Whipps (Killed in action)

(Plus probably, Sgt L S Smith, for a short period.)

*During 'Battle of Briatin'

Nominal Roll of Pilots, February 1944

RAF, British

Sq Ldr R A Sutherland DFC (CO)
Flt Lt F G Wooley DFC
Flt Lt K L Charney
Flt Lt W G Bennets
Flt Lt J O Carpenter
Fg Off R H C Thomerson
Fg Off D R Hall
Fg Off A R Stewart
Fg Off M W Frith
Fg Off A W Manson
Plt Off J B Spence
Plt Off W M L Remlinger
Plt Off I Blair DFM
Plt Off J W Kelly
Flt Sgt R W Hook
Flt Sgt L G Baggett
Flt Sgt C H Jenkins
Flt Sgt J S McConachie
Flt Sgt F J Fox

Canadian

Fg Off A P Robson
Plt Off R J Gourlay
Plt Off F S Sorge

Australian

Plt Off B J Dumbrell

New Zealander

Fg Off M D Morgan
Fg Off B J Alner

Allied

Cpt P G J Aubertin (Free French)
Cpt P H Clostermann (Free French)
Flt Sgt W M L Remlinger

The City of Glasgow Squadron had gone truly international!

Squadron pilots at the end of the War (RAF Coltishall, April 1945)

Sq Ldr R A (Max) Sutherland DFC and Bar (CO)
Flt Lt Z Wroblewski VM CdeG (Polish)
Flt Lt A O Pullman
Flt Lt W M Campbell
Flt Lt J N Hubbard
Flt Lt R F Baxter
Flt Lt G D Stephenson
Fg Off W J H Roberts
Fg Off D Hannah
Fg Off H H McHardy (New Zealand)
Fg Off S G Kingent
Fg Off C J Züber
Plt Off J Toome
Plt Off M V Francis
WO J M Annes
WO S Sollitt

WO R W Hook
WO R M Baerlin
WO L T Menzies
WO M Ellis
Flt Sgt T Love
Flt Sgt S Gomm

With the ground crews, without whose great efforts little could have been achieved. These were the men who wrote the final wartime chapter of 602. Attacking the V2 sites and dive-bombing enemy targets across the Channel.

Post-War, 1946-1957

Officers
(*—Served Pre-war)

90161	Robinson M*, AFC	1/9/46
90164	Urie J D*	12/46
90170	Jack D M*	12/46
91253	Reid R I	
91256	Robinson A W, DFC	12/2/47
91257	Young J N W	
91275	Stewart T F	7/3/47
91302	Yuille J	
91288	Richardson A	
163749	McWilliam H	
67727	Reid R N	29/6/48
151396	Melling W H	20/10/47
187680	Forrest J A	3/12/48
180333	Brown D G P	3/12/48
109942	Brown A W	11/12/48
112356	MacGregor W B	31/3/49
103601	Wright T L	25/5/49
185547	Johnston J A, DFC	11/2/50
109548	Bowd J E	12/4/50
55006	Askins K T B	9/5/50
195825	Ross E G	6/6/50
2600125	Paxton I A	10/7/50
78851	Stephen H M, DSO DFC	9/6/50
2444460	Elliott D G	6/10/51
110227	Hilson S L	9/4/52

500597	Bryson J R	16/4/52
2498688	Gilbert W M	21/12/52
2502530	Agnew W M	1/2/53
2683011	MacGuire J	31/10/52
2683013	Hogg I E	31/10/52
2504899	Davies A	23/2/53
205188	Gray W S M	11/1/53
2515976	McNab W W	9/6/53
2683071	McAllister W J	31/7/53
2683111	Daly J V P	31/7/53
51112	Barron T	30/11/53
3135585	McKay K A	1/2/54
196184	Farquhar W	10/5/54
91388	Fisher D N	1/6/54
2520706	Winchester W	10/10/54
2548225	Smith J C	10/10/54
3139343	Philip R A D	31/1/55
2683116	Bowman A H	14/12/54
2683141	Galloway W W	16/12/54
2683142	MacLean N M	16/10/54
2683148	Wilson J M	16/10/54
2583661	Rosenfeld K J	7/3/55
3140725	Brackenridge J B	3/7/55
2708932	Lockwood P B	8/11/55
2600498	Fletcher W	30/11/55
2709392	Scott W A	15/11/55
2718065	Middleton S M	29/3/56
2600526	Bell P B	?/56
2600527	Caie A G R	9/10/56
2733451	Reid J	10/10/56
2737941	Carson R G	6/12/56

Airmen
(*—Served Pre-war)

		1947
2683300	Hamilton A W	30/1
301	Reid A P	,,
302	Paterson J	,,
303	Henderson H J*	5/2
304	McKinnon W*	,,
305	Richard P*	,,
306	Mitchell J	8/2
307	Lake J E	,,
308	Melling W H	,,
309	Forrest J A	,,
310	Russell R H	13/2
311	Schooling C J	,,
312	Boe W	,,
313	Brown W H S	,,
314	Rae G S*	,,
315	Mooney J*	18/5
316	Banks J H	15/2
317	Davis A F	20/2
318	McDowell A	,,
319	Hartley J	,,
320	Taylor A F	24/2
2683000	Guy J	29/2
001	O'Neill W	1/6
002	Riley K S	8/6
003	Bryson D G	21/6
004	Law W	,,
005	Clements S H	22/6
006	Alexander J	,,
007	Gray G C	,,
008	Currie W	,,
009	McVey J S	,,
010	Watt W	26/6
011	McGuire J	15/7
012	Carmichael L G	2/10
013	Hogg I E	,,
014	McIntosh J	9/10
015	McIntosh A	,,
016	Blair R N	16/10
017	Donaldson J	,,
018	Kirk I F	11/12
019	Benjamin N	,,
020	McPhee A	,,
		1948
2683021	Headley G	17/1
022	Cameron G	,,
023	Scott J	14/2
024	Butler J	18/3
025	Clark A	,,
026	Gilmour R	,,
027	Gray D C	13/3
028	Horne J D	18/3
029	Thomson D	25/3

No.	Name	Date	No.	Name	Date	No.	Name	Date
030	Ballantyne R	17/4	072	Sutherland E	,,	114	Cunningham D	,,
031	Boyd J	16/4	073	MacLeod J	25/11	115	Craig I	,,
032	Hastings A	25/4	074	McVey J E	9/12	116	Bowman A H	9/7
033	Paterson A S	24/4	075	Stewart A R	16/12	117	Rafferty P	30/4
034	Murphy R	25/4	076	Biedie W A	18/12	118	Bell R	25/5
035	Ritchie J	13/5		**1949**		119	Hart W D	,,
036	Greenslade F	20/5	077	Whitaker W	9/1	120	O'Donnell A	,,
037	Larkin W F	,,	078	Connelly W	16/1	121	Kennedy S	11/6
038	McFadyen J	,,	079	Mortimer A G	17/2	122	McNulty J	,,
039	Scott F A	22/5	080	Crosher J G R	13/3	123	Bathgate J	1/10
040	Steele G H	,,	081	McArthur A	,,	124	Chester M	,,
041	Stewart R	23/5	082	Agnew G D N	,,	125	Kiggins J	,,
042	Watson W	,,	083	Frash F J	,,	126	Sparks C	5/10
043	Ross W	,,	084	Harrison W H	20/3	127	Grinis R J F	29/10
044	Dick J	6/6	085	Laird J A	10/4	128	Young A C	10/12
045	McColl R J	30/5	086	Kerr H T	31/3	5004700	Porteous R	19/10
046	Johnston J A	6/6	087	Flincy T A	,,	5004701	Ritchie J	29/10
047	Meldrum W R	20/6	088	Dunsmuir A	,,	2683129	Harvie W	14/12
048	Christie A C	,,	089	Perry J	,,		**1951**	
049	Kilpatrick J	20/5	090	Lennon J	,,	2683130	Farrell J	11/2
050	McIntosh D	27/6	091	Wilson H	,,	5004702	Boithwick G	7/9
051	Shields D M	,,	092	Morton D S	,,	5044703	Whigham J	23/9
052	Watt H B	,,	093	Caldwell T	2/4	2683131	Leonard E	21/10
053	Chisholm D M	3/7	094	McCairns C	3/4	132	Forster R	1/11
054	McAulay	15/7	095	Kinnell W K	,,	133	Ross W M	,,
055	Edlerman	11/7	096	Arnott J	28/4	134	Robertson J F	,,
056	Taylor J	29/8	097	Jamieson D J	,,		**1952**	
057	Campbell K	30/8	098	Moir S T W	19/5	135	Coffield W	23/3
058	Martin J W M	30/9	099	Smith J C	11/9	136	Stordy J M	,,
059	Sorbie J	3/10	100	Dick A	22/9	137	Stevens C M	20/4
060	Todd A	,,	101	MacFarlane S	13/10	138	Mogan P	24/4
	1949		102	Meldrum J	13/10	139	Brownlie G	27/4
061	McLucas J	1/5	103	Park J	4/12	140	Ritchie R	8/6
	1948			**1950**		5004704	Gray T	13/7
062	Dawson J A	7/10	104	Blyth A T	15/1	2683141	Galloway W W	14/9
063	Lawrence J	17/10	105	Brennan G	19/1	142	MacLean N M	8/6
064	McIntyre W B	21/10	106	Dick J	2/2	143	Hurry R	13/7
065	Jack R	,,	107	Branston T	26/2	144	Jones K	14/9
066	Wilson J	,,	108	McFadyen A C	2/3	145	McIntyre G	8/6
067	Colman J	4/11	109	Walker R F W	26/3	146	MacFarlane T	30/10
068	Connolly J	,,	110	McKay A	17/6	147	Barnsdale R	8/11
069	Connolly J	,,	111	Daly J V P	30/3	148	Wilson H J A	12/10
070	MacLean H	,,	112	Shaw A	16/4	149	Murray H	23/10
071	McAllister W J	11/11	113	Cameron J	,,	150	Brown R	,,

151	McKay N F	27/11	
152	Colman E	14/12	
153	Narham G	,,	
154	Thorn J	,,	
155	Taylor H	,,	
		1953	
2683156	McBride G	15/1	
5004705	Clark J	29/3	
2683157	Rigby J	23/4	
158	Morrison J	31/1	
159	Flemington R	26/4	
160	Downie A	,,	
5004706	Calder J	,,	
2677540	Wilson J	1/7	
2683161	Giblin P	26/4	
162	Stanford R	30/5	
163	Young J	21/6	
164	McAllister A	19/9	
165	Campbell G	8/11	
166	Ross J	20/12	
		1954	
2683167	Fraser A	24/1	
5004707	Kelbie W	,,	
708	Miller R F	28/2	
2683168	Sloan W T	4/3	
169	Blue W A	7/3	
170	Traynow P	13/3	
171	MacGregor M E	,,	
172	Cochran W	14/3	
173	Maclachlan J	18/3	
5004710	Simpson A	20/3	
2683174	Quinn C R	21/3	

5004711	Anderson A	27/3	
2683175	Ronald R	28/3	
176	Mouland H S	,,	
177	Campbell W	11/4	
178	Gray P T	14/3	
179	Perkins J	2/4	
180	Sweeney T	,,	
181	Heft P B	,,	
182	Paterson J B	8/5	
183	Gillespie W	,,	
184	Young R	9/5	
185	Hutchison J	,,	
802568	Rae G	,,	
2427154	Casey A	,,	
2683187	Ewart R B	30/5	
188	Smith T W	,,	
189	Fotheringham R	6/6	
2559706	Grunslade F	13/6	
2605759	Watson J	3/7	
2605844	Chambers W	11/9	
2683190	Booth J	12/9	
191	Johnstone A	,,	
193	Cochran W	17/10	
1126383	McKenzie A	18/11	
2683194	MacFarlane B	20/11	
186	Callachan J	31/10	
4022873	Galloway J	21/11	
549578	Thomson S M	28/11	
631180	Lee G	28/11	
		1955	
2683195	Stewart J	11/1	
196	Spy A	30/1	

197	Eckford J	,,	
198	Brodie W	,,	
199	Roberts B	13/2	
200	Spelling J	20/3	
201	Muir C	3/4	
202	Sellers J	3/4	
4020593	Gibson D	24/4	
2683203	Ritchie M	1/5	
204	Cairns	,,	
205	Cross B	25/6	
2454680	Dowling A	19/6	
2511541	Armstrong R	15/10	
1105080	Dodds D J	19/6	
2683206	Pattison A	16/10	
207	Campbell A	6/11	
208	McCaw T H	11/12	
		1956	
2683209	Macdonald B S	5/2	
210	Russell J P	,,	
1482357	Manning R J	19/2	
1345860	Waigh H	11/3	
2488211	Hunter D C	25/3	
212	Philips I	22/4	
213	Dime D	6/5	
4029162	Park G T	28/4	
2504960	Coshett G S	5/6	
3062976	Foy M	20/5	
3136931	Clarkson J	1/9	
2683214	Kerr J	2/9	
215	Flood J	,,	
2721967	Downie W	4/11	
2722296	Anderon L J	4/11	
3122186	Duncan R S	16/12	

The names of personnel serving on the Squadron during the war years have been purposely omitted due to the considerable difficulties in obtaining, this information. Some were posted in from other Auxiliary Squadrons but, with the embodiment of the Auxiliary Air Force into the RAF at the beginning of the war, most would have been enlisted under the RAFVR.

The Regulars

Each Auxiliary Squadron was originally established with a nucleus of regular RAF personnel including a few officers—the Adjutant, Assistant Adjutant (training officer) and, at least initially, Stores or Admin Officer, viz. Mitchell and Redman in the early days.

602 in common with its fellow Auxiliary Squadron was served by a number of distinguished RAF officers including of course its CO for the first few months, Squadron Leader C N Lowe MC DFC, who went on to command 43 (Fighter) Squadron, 'The Fighting Cocks'.

The Auxiliary squadrons as a whole were fortunate in the choice of regular officers selected to serve with them in the above key posts.

602 was certainly well favoured and enjoyed the services of some very fine officers.

'Dan' Martyn, who kicked them off with his assistant Finney were to be followed by messrs. Whitford, Bennett, Barwell (shot down by friendly aircraft whilst commanding the Biggin Hill Wing during the Battle of Britain), Vere-Harvey, Powell, Critchley, Mathieson, 'Stacy' Hodson, who became as Air Vice Marshal), and 'Mark' Selway who retired as Air Chief Marshal Sir Anthony Selway. Finally, in the pre-war period, Messrs. Dale, Darley and Hodder.

Post-war, first to arrive on reformation was the Regular RAF Adjutant Flt Lt D O Cunliffe DFC, shortly to be followed by Flt Lt M W Grierson-Jackson, Assistant Adjutant and Training Officer. They were followed by Flight Lieutenants, J Muir, A A V Maxwell, Johnson, A Powell, F Morris, H D Costain, R A McPhie, R C Bridges, R McGowan and J I Walker, together with Regular Engineering Officers, Flight Lieutenants Hume, Beedie, Gough, Logan, Barron and MacFarlane all supported by a contingent of Regular NCOs and Airmen without whom . . .

APPENDIX II

ORGANISATION AND CONTROL

Light Bomber Squadron
15 September 1925—31 October 1938
Air Defence of Great Britain, Special Reserve and Auxiliary Air Force, renamed No.1 Air Defence Group, ADGB on 25th August 1927.
No.6 (Auxiliary) Group from 1st April 1936 within the newly instituted Bomber Command from 14th July 1936.
No.2 (Bomber) Group from February 1937

Army Co-operation Squadron
1st November 1938—13th January 1939
No.22 Group

Fighter Squadron
14th January 1939—15th May 1945 and
11th June 1946—10th March 1957
Fighter Command
No.12 (Fighter) Group
No.13 (Fighter) Group
No.11 (Fighter) Group
2nd Tactical Air Force,
No.83 Group, 125 Wing from 13th November 1943
Fighter Command
Returned to the U.K. from October 1944—15th May 1945
Reserve Command
No.66 (Scottish) Reserve Group, 11th June 1946—31st October 1949
Fighter Command
No.12 (Fighter) Group, 'Caledonian' Sector, 1st November 1949—October 1955.
No.13 (Fighter) Group, October 1955—10th March 1957.

Command Organisation 1946-1957
602, in common with all other Auxiliary Squadrons, came under RAF Reserve Command with Headquarters at White Waltham although operated locally under 66 (Scottish) Reserve Group at Turnhouse. In November 1949, the flying squadrons of the Royal Auxiliary Air Force were transferred to Fighter Command and 602 became one of 12 Group's squadrons within the 'Caledonian' or 'Scottish' Sector. The other elements of the Scottish Sector were 502 (County of Ulster) Squadron, 603 (City of Edinburgh) Squadron and 612 (County of Aberdeen) Squadron.

Scottish Auxiliary Wing Leaders (Post War)

(Position filled by the Station Commander/Wing Commander Flying at RAF Turnhouse). Scottish Auxiliary Wing comprised 602, 603 and 612 Squadrons.

—Wg Cdr G L Millington DFC
—Wg Cdr W G G Duncan Smith DSO DFC, March 1953—July 1955
—Wg Cdr A L Winskill DFC, July 1955—January 1957 (Subsequently became Captain of the Queen's Flight).
—Wg Cdr R C Haine DFC, January 1957—March 1957.

AIRCRAFT

D.H.9A

7th October 1925-January 1928

H144 (Squadron's first aircraft)
J7020
J7863
BASE: Renfrew

COLOUR SCHEMES: Silver with black serials. No known sqn mks.
N.B. Because of Renfrew's restricted space, these a/c had modified u/c oleos.

Avro 504K

October 1925-1927

F8808
F8866
H9832
BASE: Renfrew

COLOUR SCHEMES: None known, no information available.

Avro 504N

From January 1927

E9357
H236
H2975 (con 504K) w/o in mid-air coll with Wapiti J9602, 7/3/31. Both pilots, Land and Phillips, killed, observer/gunner A/C Eddie Smith parachuted to safety.
H9871
J8508

J8509
J8678
J8679
J9253 '2'
J9255
J9705
J9706
K1806
K1982 cd into hills 15/9/36
K1983 o/t ldg 7/3/35. Pilot A M Grant unhurt. SOC.
K2347
K2371
K2376
K2401
K2421

BASES: Renfrew and Abbotsinch

COLOUR SCHEMES: Silver with black serials. '602' in flight colours (possibly some this in black). Original 602 Sqn badge on some a/c.
J8508 had a long blue band along fuselage.
J8509 had a long wide red band along fuselage.
K1982 repainted in yellow training scheme in 1935, others may also have been similarly painted.

Fairey Fawn I/II/III

September 1927-June 1930

Fawn I
J7182 (Mk.I)
J7183 (Mk.I)

J7185 (Mk.II)
J7188 (Mk.II) cd ldg Renfrew 16/6/28. Pilot D F McIntyre unhurt.
J7190 (Mk.II) '2' ('bars'—possibly red—either side of fuselage roundel)
J7200 (Mk.II)
J7212 (Mk.II)
J7219 (Mk.II)
J7222 (Mk.II)
J7229 (Mk.II)
J7769 (Mk.III)
J7770 (Mk.III)
J7981 (Mk.III)
J7985 (Mk.III)

BASE: Renfrew

COLOUR SCHEMES: Silver with black serials. No known sqn mks. Three a/c initially del 9/27. At the annual camp at Leuchars in 1928 there were "six Fawns plus four Avros". The last three were flown to Hawkinge in 6/30.

Westland Wapiti I/IIA

31st July 1929-February 1934

J9094 (Mk.I) w/o in grd coll with J9602 at Leuchars 29/7/30.
J9595
J9596
J9597
J9598
J9600
J9601

J9602 w/o in grd coll with J9094 at Leuchars 29/7/30. Pilot D F McIntyre unhurt.

J9603 w/o in mid-air coll with Avro 504N, H2975, 7/3/31.

J9618
J9860
J9862
J9863
J9867
J9868
J9871
K1143
K1156
K1316
K1317

BASES: Renfrew, Abbotsinch.

COLOUR SCHEMES: Silver overall with dark green ('nivo') or black top decking (individual variations). '602' and wheel covers in flight colours ('A' Flt, red; 'B' Flt yellow; 'C' Flt blue).'602' outlined in black at some time—varying sizes. Original sqn badge on fin.

Westland Wapiti VI (Trainer)
August 1931-1934

K2239

BASES: Renfrew, Abbotsinch

COLOUR SCHEMES: As for Wapiti IIAs. '602' possibly in blue.

N.B. Squadron strength was "eleven Wapitis plus three Avros", eight Wapitis being on on charge by September 1929.

Hawker Hart I
February 1934-June 1936

K1420
K3044
K3054
K3857

K3858
K3859 cd 24/2/35
K3861
K3862
K3865
K3866 fce/ld Portobello, 24/2/35, en route to AuxAF rugby match. Pilot A D Farquhar 'C' Flight. Same occasion as 3859 and 3875.
K3869
K3870
K3875 fce/ld Craigiehall, 24/2/35. Pilot P/O J Shewell.
K3877
K3878
K3880
K3897
K3965

BASE: Abbotsinch

COLOUR SCHEMES: Silver, some without fin flashes. '602' in flight colours. Original sqn badge on fin.

Hawker Hart Trainer
From May 1937

K3749 Silver finish.
K6522 Yellow finish.

BASE: Abbotsinch

D.H.60M Gipsy Moth
During 1935

K1112 Flown by 602 Sqn pilots (i.e. Marquess of Douglas & Clydesdale).

Hawker Hind
June 1936-November 1938

K5418
K5460
K5500
K5502

K5503
K5504
K5505
K5506
K5507
K5508
K5509
K5510 Hit telephone wires on ldg at Rochford (Southend) during annual camp, 27/7/37. Pilot J Hawkes unhurt.
K5511
K5513

BASE: Abbotsinch

COLOUR SCHEMES: Silver overall, no fin flashes. Later, bold '602' in red on all? a/c plus version of new sqn badge in 'grenade' (official Bomber Command design) on fin. Wheel centres also coloured as per '602'

Hawker Hind Trainer

K4645
L7229

BASE: Abbotsinch

COLOUR SCHEMES: Yellow overall trainer finish

Avro Tutor
July 1936-September 1939

K3305
K3354 w/o in fce/ldg 10/8/36.
K3446 cr fce/ldg Airdrie, 25/4/38.
K6097 Abbotsinch Stn Flt, but used by 602 Sqn.

BASE: Abbotsinch

COLOUR SCHEMES: Thought to be yellow overall trainer finish.

Hawker Hector
November 1938-January 1939

K9733
K9734
K9749
K9750
K9751
K9752
K9753
K9754
K9755
K9756
K9757
K9761
K9765
K9770
K9777
K9778

BASE: Abbotsinch

COLOUR SCHEMES: Probably silver overall but no photographic reference available. In view of the very short time these a/c were on strength it is unlikely that any sqn mks were applied.

Gloster Gauntlet II
January 1939-May 1939

K5287
K5288
K5293
K5301
K5305
K5309
K5319
K5352
K5354
K5364
K7813
K7833
K7837
K7841
K7858   Possibly LO-E
K7865
K7869

K7873
K7879   LO-K

BASE: Abbotsinch

COLOUR SCHEMES: From the only known photograph it appears that these a/c were camouflage dark green and dark earth with black and white undersides. Sqn ident letters 'LO' plus individual code letter. The Empire Air Day order of 1939 identifies these a/c by letter. It would seem that 602 initially used 'LO' on the Gauntlets but changed to 'ZT' when the first Spitfires arrived.

Fairey Battle II
March 1939-June 1940

N2102
N2103

BASES: Abbotsinch, Drem

COLOUR SCHEMES: Std RAF camouflage of dark green and dark earth with black undersides. Black serials on rear fuselage and rudder.
N.B. These a/c were allocated for pilot familiarisation purposes in preparation for Spitfires.

Supermarine Spitfire I/Ia
8 May 1939-June 1941

The initial batch of 19 a/c were allotted to the Squadron on 26 April 1939 with first deliveries to Abbotsinch being made on 8 May. They were flown direct from the Vickers-Supermarine production line at Woolston (Southampton) and arrived devoid of guns, armour plate or oxygen system all of which was subsequently installed. 602 was equipped with Sptifires in advance of many of the RAF's regular squadrons which were then still flying biplanes. It was, in fact. the first Auxiliary and eighth squadron in the Air Force to receive this most advanced aircraft.

North American Harvard I
From October 1939

P5867

BASES: Abbotsinch, Drem and possibly elsewhere.

COLOUR SCHEMES: Std RAF cam with yellow trainer mks. No 602 mks.

D.H.82A, Tiger Moth II
From May 1940

N6930
EM908 'LO'   Used during 1943-44

BASES: Drem and others.

COLOUR SCHEMES: No details available. Probably std trainer colours.

Miles M.14A Magister.
From June 1940

L8161   Abbotsinch Stn Flt. Used by 602 Sqn.
R1915   At Ayr and Kenley, August 1941
T9873

BASES: Abbotsinch, Drem, Westhampnett, Prestwick, Ayr.

COLOUR SCHEMES: L8161 and R1915 in std trainer colour—no 602 mks.

K9961 del. 10/5/39, ZT-M?/LO-M 'Dopey'.

K9962 del. 8/5/39, ZT-A?/LO-A. A D Farquhar's a/c, o/t in field after beside downed He111 which he had s/dn, 22/2/40.

K9963 del. 8/5/39.

K9964 del. 10/5/39, ZT-B?/LO-B 'Bogus'. Miles Master flew into this a/c on the ground, 16/5/40. Hector MacLean unhurt.

K9965 del. 10/5/39. cr nr Glasgow on night training flight, 8/9/39. SOC 3/10/39.

K9966 del. 12/3/39, ZT-E. Crashed when u/c collapsed on t/o, Abbotsinch, 8/7/39. SOC 15/8/39.

K9967 del. 10/5/39, ZT-O. Dam in w/u ldg. To Morris Motors for rep (their first), 30/5/39.

K9968 del. 8/5/39. Cr/ld nr Cherbourg, 21/11/39.

K9969 del. 8/5/39, /LO-L, (3/40). Hit by Bf109 and further dam in cr/ldg by coll with Poling RDF mast, 18/8/40. Pilot P J Ferguson wounded and suffered shock.

K9970 del. 8/5/39, ZT-D? /LO-D, (9/39). Cr in fce/ldg nr West Kilbride, due to e/fld, 6/1/41.

K9971 del. 8/5/39, ZT-P, O/s on ldg Church Fenton during annual camp, 18/7/39. Pilot Norman Stone unhurt.

K9972 del. 16/5/39.

K9973 del. 16/5/39, ZT-Q/LO-Q 'Bashful', Sandy Johnstone's a/c. Cd at night nr West Kilbride after being scrambled in very poor weather, 30/9/39-1/10/39. Johnstone unhurt.

K9974 del. 15/5/39, ZT-H?/LO-H, (11/39). Coll with L1079 at Drem 26/11/39.

K9975 del. 18/5/39, ZT-R?/LO-R, (11/39).

K9976 del. 18/5/39.

K9977 del. 18/5/39, /LO-P, (12/39).

K9978 del. 18/5/39, ZT-G?/LO-G, (10/39, 3/40), Ran-out of fuel. Cd nr Dunbar, 2/3/40.

K9979 del. 22/5/39.

Even before the outbreak of the war on 3/9/39, a few replacement a/c had been delivered.

The Squadron was initially divided into two flights each of which were further sub-divided into sections of three aircraft. Sections were identified by colour, 'A' Flight having 'Red' and 'Blue' and 'B' Flight 'Green' and 'Yellow'. 'B' Flight aircraft were also given the names of Disney's famous Seven Dwarfs!

Subsequent deliveries:

K9833 del. 20/1/40

K9839 del. 23/1/40, LO-Q. Dbf from Do17 and cr/ld west of Wrothan, 7/9/40. Pilot E W Aries unhurt.

K9881 del. 24/3/40. Dam in act with Ju87, 16/8/40. Pilot T G F Ritchie unhurt.

K9890 del. 13/7/40.

K9892 del. 29/11/39, LO-N. A/c was 'blessed' by Padre Sutherland at Drem in July 1940 together with a 605 Sqn Hurricane. Spitfire cr Drem in night ldg in mist. Pilot H W Moody unhurt. (The Hurricane also crashed thereafter).

K9899 del. 24/3/40 LO-H (5/40).

K9933 del. 28/11/39, LO-H (12/39). Dam ldg Drem, 9/1/40. Pilot A M Grant unhurt.

K9955 del. 8/11/39. Dam ops, fce/ld 4/9/40.

K9995 del. 19/8/40, Believed dam by He59. Pilot safe.

L1002 LO-D (12/39), LO-B (3/40), LO-D (6/40). 'Ogo-Pogo'. Dunlop Urie's a/c. Dam fce/ldg Tangmere, 10/9/40. Pilot O V Hanbury unhurt.

L1004 del. 24/9/39 LO-Q, 'Kedoying'. Sandy Johnstone's a/c replacing K9973. Dam on grd during raid on Tangmere 16/8/40 (in hanger under maintenance). Rep and conv to Mk.Va and later became prototype P.R. Mk.XIII.

L1005 del. 24/9/39, LO-F, 'Donald Duck', Donald Jack's a/c. Sev dam in act with Ju87 and Bf109 over Ford 18/8/40. Pilot C J Mount unhurt. A/c rep.

L1018 del. 17/6/39, LO-J

L1019 del. 24/6/39 ZT-G?/LO-S (10/39, 4/40) 'Grumpy'. Flown by G C Pinkerton on 16th October 1939 during the first Fighter Command actions of WWII. In the morning he attacked and damaged a He111 of KG26 and in the afternoon he shot down a Ju88 of KG30—both actions over the Forth. L1019 was subsequently shot down nr Portsmouth 18/8/40. Pilot B E P Whall safe.

L1027 del. 21/12/39, LO-A (4/40). Not highly regarded as witness its caricature—known as the 'Flying Shithouse'. S/dn by Bf110 11/9/40. Pilot S N Rose, wounded.

L1031

L1040 del. 10/7/39, LO-E, (11/39). Dam by Ju88 and Bf109's over Dungeness, 31/8/40. Cr/ld nr Bognor 10/9/40. Pilot Elcombe safe.

L1079 del. 18/8/39, LO-N (11/39). Coll with K9974 at Drem 26/11/39, SOC 12/1/40.

N3109 del. 24/12/39, LO-J (3/40).

N3119 del. 14/3/40.

N3164 del. 4/12/39.

N3165 del. 27/12/39. Dam 27/5/40, SOC 14/6/40.

N3166 LO-H?

N3190 del. 3/5/40. Aban over Pentland Hills 26/6/40.

N3198 del. 6/8/40. S/dn by Bf109 over Tunbridge Wells, 7/9/40. Pilot W H Coverley seriously injured and subsequently died.

N3226 del. 7/4/40. S/dn by Bf109s near Dorchester, 28/8/40. Pilot M H Sprague baled-out and rescued from sea.

N3227 del. 7/4/40. Shot-down by Bf109s over Hailsham, 6/9/40. Pilot G A Whipps safe.

N3228 del. 7/4/40, LO-X, (6/40). Dam by Do17 over South London, 7/9/40. Pilot O V Hanbury unhurt.

N3236 del. 3/5/40.

N3242 del. 13/9/40.

N3249 del. 10/11/40.

N3270 del. 7/3/41.

N3282 del. 19/8/40. S/dn by Bf110s over Channel 11/9/40. Pilot M H Sprague killed.

P9311 del. 17/12/40.

P9328 del. 20/5/40.

P9381 del. 13/7/40. S/dn near Dorchester, 25/8/40. Pilot W H Coverley baled-out, unhurt.

P9439 del. 14/12/40.

P9446 Rtd dam by Ju88, 12/10/40. Pilot J S Hart unhurt.

P9461 del. 3/6/40, LO-B. Cr during night ldg in mist at Drem, 1/8/40. Pilot J D Urie unhurt.

P9510 del. 13/7/40. Dam by Ju88 over Selsey Bill, 30/9/40. Pilot J S Hart unhurt.

P9515 del. 27/8/40. Dam by Bf109 at Mayfield, 30/10/40. Pilot A Lyall safe.

P9463 del. 2/6/40. Dam in act by Ju87s at Tangmere, 16/8/40. Pilot H W Moody safe.

P9469 del. 20/5/40.

R6600   del. 19/8/40. Dam by Bf109s over Hailsham, 6/9/40. Pilot P J Ferguson unhurt.

R6601   del. 20/8/40. Dam by Bf109s over Hailsham, 9/40. Pilot H W Moody unhurt.

R6612   del. 14/12/40.

R6627   del. 24/1/41, LO-E (5/41).

R6691   del. 2/5/41.

R6780   del. 13/9/40.

R6834   del. 19/8/40. Dam by Bf109s over Hailsham, 6/9/40. Pilot T G F Ritchie slightly wounded.

R6839   FTR ops, 26/10/40. Pilot D W Elcombe missing.

R6915   del. 1/41 at Prestwick. Now preserved in IWM London.

R6965   del. 31/8/40.

R6969   del. 24/12/40.

R6993   del. 14/12/40.

R7071   del. 28/4/41, 'Perseus'—one of three Spitfires presented by Sir Frederick Richmond and family.

X4012   del. 13/10/40.

X4028   del. 12/12/40.

X4030   del. 11/8/40.

X4104   del. 12/9/40.

X4110   del. 18/8/40 (morning). No code, Dunlop Urie's a/c (for a very short time!) Dbr in combat (afternoon)—operational life, 20 minutes! Urie wounded in legs, to hospital.

X4160   del. 16/8/40. Rtd to base slightly dam after mid-air coll with another Spitfire, 27/9/40. Pilot T G F Ritchie. Dam by Bf109s, 27/9/40. Pilot C F Babbage. S/dn by Ju88 at Lullington, 7/10/40. Pilot B E P Whall killed.

X4161   del. 16/8/40. Fce/ld at Ford after combat with Bf109s, burst tyre and nosed-over, 18/8/40. Pilot H W Moody safe.

X4162   del. 16/8/40. LO-J, Sandy Johnstone's a/c. Used in BofB after L1004's demise.

X4169   del. 15/8/40.

X4187   del. 21/8/40. S/dn by Bf109s of 1/JG53 and belly-landed at Tangmere 26/8/40. Pilot C H MacLean lost foot in combat, to hospital.

X4188   del. 21/8/40. S/dn by Bf109s off Bognor Regis, 26/8/40. Pilot C F Babbage to Bognor hospital.

X4239   del. 17/12/40.

X4240   del. 14/12/40.

X4245   del. 14/12/40.

X4256   del. 24/8/40. S/dn by Bf109s nr Biggin Hill, 7/9/40. Pilot H W Moody, missing.

X4263   del. 21/10/40.

X4266   del. 24/11//40. LO-F then LO-J after X4162 was damaged.

X4268   Development a/c fitted with metal ailerons and tested by Sandy Johnstone at Westhampnett on 19/11/40. Found to be very successful. Not a 602 a/c.

X4269   del. 27/8/40. Rtd dam after combat with Bf109s. Pilot C F Babbage unhurt. Fce/ld nr Dymchurch, 30/10/40. Pilot D H Gage unhurt.

X4270   del. 27/8/40. Slight dam ldg Tangmere 10/9/40. Pilot C J Mount unhurt.

X4336   del. 4/1/41.

X4382   del. 10/9/40, LO-G, (12/40)

X4389   del. 12/9/40.

X4390   del. 12/9/40.

X4411   del. 13/9/40. Rtd dbf from He111. Pilot A L Edy unhurt.

X4412   del. 13/9/40. Dbf from Do17 over Beachy Head and fce/ld at Shoreham, 15/9/40. Pilot C F Babbage unhurt.

X4414   del. 13/9/40. Dam by Bf109s and fce/ld at Mayfield, 27/9/40. Pilot D H Gage unhurt.

X4487   del. 13/1/41.

X4541   del. 2/10/40. LO-M. Dam by Ju88, cd Ford, 12/10/40. Pilot C F Babbage safe.

X4542   del. 2/10/40. S/dn by Bf109s nr Mayfield, 30/10/40. Pilot W B Smith safe. Last Spitfire to be s/dn in BofB.

X4557

X4603   del. 13/10/40. Wing-tip dam by Bf109s over Maidstone, 29/10/40. Pilot H G Niven unhurt.

X4615   del. 14/12/40.

X4623   'Scillonia'

X4648   del. 14/12/40.

X4658   del. 1/11/40.   Lost in action, 11/12/40

X4659   del. 1/11/40.

X4661   del. 9/12/40.

X4671   del. 29/11/40.

X4673   del. 17/11/40.

X4681   del. 14/12/40. Missing 24/5/41.

X4709   del. 3/1/41.

X4769   del. 21/11/40.

X4829   del. 26/2/41.

L1007 was a cannon armed aircraft 'owned' by A&AEE Boscombe Down but allocated to 605 Squadron for operational trials. 605 was then commanded by George Pinkerton who arranged for the Spitfire's transfer together with its pilot, George Proudman, to 602 at Drem early in 1940. It was usually flown as 'number two' in a section until it was damaged in a forced landing on 28/5/40.

BASES: Abbotsinch, Grangemouth, Drem, Montrose ('A' Flt), Dyce ('B' FLt), Drem, Westhampnett (Battle of Britain), Prestwick, Ayr (Heathfield). (Ayr was opened on 7 April 1941 as a Fighter Command Sector Station in 13(F) Group.)

COLOUR SCHEMES: Aircraft delivered in May 1939 were in the standard RAF camouflaged dark green and dark earth with silver, black or black and white undersides. They carried no fin flashes and had small 'B' type fuselage roundels with small serial numbers on mid fin or upper rear fuselage in front of fin (eg L1004).

Squadron identification letters 'ZT' together with individual aircraft letters were applied in medium grey. ('A' Flight using 'A' to 'K' and 'B' Flight 'M' onwards).

In late August or early September 1939 the Squadron identification letters were changed to 'LO', and, from at least early 1940, the fuselage roundels were small 'A' type red, white and blue. From 2 May 1940 yellow surrounds were added to the fuselage roundels and from 2 June 1940 undersides were painted duck-egg blue. Rear view mirrors were added from 2 June 1940 (in light of 605's experiences).

From November 1940 it can be assumed that the standard RAF schemes applied with black serial numbers on the rear fuselage becoming common.

Extract from the Operations Order for the move of 602 Sqn from Drem to Montrose ('A' Flt) and Dyce ('B' Flt) dated 14th April 1940

Spitfire

'A'	Sgt Babbage	'K'	F/Lt Boyd, 'A' Flight Commander
'D'	F/O Strong	'M'	F/O Ritchie
'B'	F/Lt Urie	'N'	Sgt Moody
'E'	F/O McLean	'P'	F/O Webb
'F'	F/O Jack	'Q'	F/Lt Johnstone, 'B' Flight Commander
'G'	Sgt MacDowall	'R'	F/O Ferguson
'J'	P/O Coverley	'S'	S/Ldr Pinkerton CO
'X'	P/O Lyall		

Also known to be on strength, 'H', F/O Grant's Aircraft.

Call Signs
'Villa 14 upwards —'A' Flight
'Villa 26 upwards —'B' Flight

Spitfire IIa
May 1941-August 1941

P7297 del. 6/7/41
P7674 del. 28/5/41
P7782 del. 11/6/41
P7818 del. 15/7/41
P7838 del. 4/7/41 'Fermanagh'
P8023 del. 15/6/41
P8047 del. 11/6/41, LO-L, 'The Malverns'
P8080 del. 1/7/41, 'Horwich'
P8183 del. 11/6/41, 'Tasmania'
P8259 del. 1/6/41
P8275 del. 11/6/41
P8375 del. 28/5/41 'Celebes'
P8396 del. 11/6/41 'Bermuda II'
P8423 del. 11/6/41
P8472 del. 7/7/41
P8478 del. 17/7/41, missing 21/7/41
P8572 del. 17/7/41, cd 9/8/41
P8577

BASES: Ayr (Heathfield), Kenley.

Spitfire Vb
July 1941-September/October 1943

K9825 del. 10/9/42, acc Peterhead
P7505 del. 10/9/42
P8718 del. 2/8/41
P8719 del. 31/7/41, FTR 7/8/42
P8722 del. 6/8/41, dbr 2/1/42
P8723 del. 10/8/41, cd 25/1/42

P8724 del. 2/8/41, cd 4/4/42
P8787
P8790 del. 2/8/41, FTR 21/9/41
P8791 del. 30/7/41
P8793 del. 30/7/41, FTR 16/8/41
P8799 del. 30/7/41
W3226 del. 19/4/43
W3230 del. 29/11/41
W3249 del. 23/12/42 'Baltic Exchange III'
W3253 del. 9/1/43 'Central Provinces Berar IV'
W3364 del. 25/11/41

W3382 del. 8/12/41, FTR ops 9/3/42
W3407 del. 18/8/41
W3426 del. 27/8/41
W3526 del. 1/3/41, FTR 13/3/42
W3569 del. 15/7/41
W3606 del. 16/6/41
W3622 del. 18/8/41, FTR 20/9/41
W3623 del. 16/8/41, FTR 10/10/41
W3638 del. 25/3/42 LO-D?
W3640 del. 1/8/41
W3641 del. 31/7/41
W3642 del. 10/8/41, FTR 17/9/41
W3649 del. 16/8/41 'Shepley'
W3709 del. 29/1/41
W3725 del. 28/8/41, FTR 21/9/41
W3726 del. 29/1/41
W3756 del. 28/8/41 'John Stevens' LO-E
W3798
W3822 del. 28/8/41 'Zanzibar IV'
W3853 del. 30/9/41 'Nyasaland II'
W3897 del. 25/9/41 'Nyasaland VII', FTR 13/10/41
W3898 del. 25/9/41
W3946 del. 15/5/41
W3951 del. 16/6/41
W3956 del. 14/10/41, lost 3/3/42
W3957 del. 29/11/41

AA757 del. 19/4/43, LO-V Eng cut 10 miles north of le Touquet while on bomber escort to Abbeville, 25/5/43
AA766
AA910 del. 19/4/43 LO-A
AA942 del. 5/12/41
AA979 del. 1/9/42
AB133 del. 1/9/42
AB185 del. 7/12/41
AB370 del. 15/7/42
AB781 del. 13/3/42
AB782 del. 26/9/43
AB794 del. 8/3/42
AB797 del. 14/10/41
AB844 del. 3/8/41, FTR 12/8/41
AB845 del. 29/11/41
AB846 del. 31/7/41
AB848 LO-F. Flown by Johnny Niven in Dieppe Raid 19/8/42

AB849 del. 9/8/41
AB851 del. 30/7/41
AB861 del. 2/8/41, FTR 13/10/41
AB862 del. 30/7/41
AB866 del. 14/10/41, LO-Y
AD189 del. 13/10/41, cd nr Crewkerne,
12/3/42
AD191 del. 22/7/42
AD236 del. 23/9/41, 'Bihor II'
AD362 del. 19/4/43, LO-C
AD515
AD536 del. 25/1/42
AR280 del. 26/1/42
AR281 del. 26/1/42
AR344 del. 29/11/42
AR396 del. 7/5/42
AR428 del. 30/6/43, Missing, presumed
s/dn nr Poix, 15/7/43
AR430 Coll with Mustang AP181, cd nr
Odiham, 19/4/43
AR454 del. 15/7/42
AR463 del. 26/1/43
BL288 del. 15/12/41
BL292 del. 27/6/43
BL295 del. 15/7/42
BL350 del. 29/11/42
BL368 del. 15/7/42
BL390 del. 15/8/42
BL416 del. 19/4/43, LO-I
BL439 del. 19/4/43, 'St Lucia Windward
Islands'
BL544 del. 16/4/43
BL548 del. 26/1/42
BL551 del. 29/11/42
BL575 del. 21/5/42
BL655 del. 15/7/42
BL666 del. 29/11/42
BL712 del. 19/4/43, LO-X
BL725 del. 21/7/43
BL734 del. 15/7/42
BL759 del. 15/7/42
BL763 del. 19/4/43
BL822
BL830 del. 29/11/42
BL862 del. 25/1/43
BL887 del. 15/7/42
BL920 del. 15/7/42
BL928 del. 25/3/43

BL932 del. 15/7/42, FTR 19/8/42
BL937 del. 15/7/42, cd 17/8/42
BL965
BL971 del. 19/4/43
BM113 del. 26/3/42
BM114 del. 18/3/42, FTR 17/5/42
BM124 del. 16/3/42, 'Queen Salote', LO-W
BM126 del. 26/3/42
BM128 del. 25/3/42
BM133 del. 15/7/42
BM136 del. 26/3/42
BM139 del. 27/3/42
BM141 del. 26/3/42
BM142 del. 19/3/42
BM147 del. 28/3/42
BM148 del. 25/3/42, Missing, Calais,
28/3/42
BM154 del. 20/6/42
BM155 del. 27/3/42, 'Joe and Roy (Davies
Bros Ltd)'
BM156 del. 25/3/42
BM157 del. 18/3/42
BM160 del. 25/3/42, 'Assam IX'
BM161 del. 25/3/42, 'Butafogo (Rio de
Janeiro)', dam, 6/5/42
BM182 del. 26/3/42, FTR, 13/7/42
BM186 del. 24/3/42, dam, 1/5/42
BM187 del. 23/3/42, s/dn 25/4/42
BM196 del. 27/3/42, 'Borough of
Brentford and Chiswick', FTR,
9/5/42
BM201 del. 3/4/42
BM204 del. 2/5/42
BM228 del. 25/3/42
BM235 del. 8/4/42, s/dn, 26/5/42
BM236 del. 29/5/42, 'Fellowship of the
Bellows, Columbia', FTR, 26/6/42
BM240 del. 9/6/42, 'Clifton Cinemas'
BM245 del. 27/3/42
BM302 del. 29/11/42
BM310 del. 29/11/42, dbr 30/12/42
BM325 del. 24/5/42, 'The Canadian
Policeman'
BM355 del. 13/5/42
BM385 del. 27/4/42
BM402 del. 11/6/42
BM426 del. 13/5/42, s/dn 17/5/42

BM451 del. 15/7/42, cd during Dieppe
raid, 19/8/42
BM456 del. 27/4/42
BM457 del. 15/7/42
BM469 del. 13/5/42, FTR 8/6/42
BM487 del. 29/11/42
BM493 del. 13/5/43, LO-S
BM510 del. 15/7/43
BM521 del. 10/6/42, spun-in 17/6/42
BM524 del. 7/5/42, cd 22/5/42
BM529 del. 21/7/42
BM568 del. 29/11/42
BM571 del. 15/7/42, cd 27/7/42
BM642 del. 31/5/43
BM645 del. 23/8/43
BM649 del. 29/11/42
BR391 del. 25/1/43

EN768 del. 29/6/42
EN840 del. 19/4/43, LO-O
EN866 del. 29/11/42
EN904 del. 15/7/42, Flown by P M
Brothers on Dieppe Raid
EN949 del. 29/11/42

EP109 del. 4/8/43
EP110 del. 24/6/42
EP113 del. 29/6/42
EP121 del. 7/3/43
EP181 del. 18/12/42
EP227 del. 11/9/42
EP244 del. 15/7/42
EP249 del. 16/7/42
EP278 del. 29/6/42
EP280 del. 8/7/42
EP380 del. 13/5/43, LO-B
EP384 del. 14/5/43
EP564 del. 7/3/42

BASES: Kenley, Redhill, Kenley, Peterhead,
Biggin Hill (for Dieppe raid), Peterhead,
Skeabrae (detachment at Sumburgh),
Perranporth, Lasham, Fairlop, Bognor,
Kingsnorth, Newchurch.

Spitfire Va

September 1942—January 1943

L1031
P7308   del. 10/9/42
P8167   del. 10/9/42
R7127   del. 10/9/42, 'Turris Jehova
        Fortissmo'
R7220   del. 10/9/42
R7302   del. 10/9/42
R7337   del. 8/3/42
W3114   del. 10/9/42
W3138   del. 10/9/42
X4173   del. 10/9/42
X4709   del. 10/9/42
BASES: Peterhead, Skeabrae, Sumburgh

Spitfire H.F.VI

September 1942-January 1943

AB527   del. 10/9/42
BR252   del. 27/10/42
BR297   del. 10/9/42
BR298   del. 10/9/42
BR304   del. 10/9/42
BR577   del. 10/9/42
BR979   del. 10/9/42
BS141   del. 14/9/42
BS146   del. 25/9/42
BS436   del. 24/9/42
BS437   del. 26/9/42
BS442   del. 24/9/42
BS472   del. 17/11/42
BASE: Skeabrae

Spitfire Vc

September 1942-April 1943

EE622   del. 19/10/42
EE627   del. 19/10/42
EE631   del. 21/10/42
EE637   del. 21/10/42
EE638   del. 7/11/42
EE643   del. 9/11/42
EE644   del. 31/10/42
EE659   del. 19/10/42
EE661   del. 21/10/42
EE665   del. 17/1/43
EE666   del. 25/1/43
EE681   del. 25/1/43

EE682   del. 17/1/43, air coll with EE633, cd
        in sea, 23/1/43
EE686   del. 25/1/43
EE687   del. 25/1/43, cd Lizard, 23/1/43
EE714   del. 25/1/43
EE717   del. 25/1/43
EE720   del. 25/1/43
EE721   del. 25/1/43
EE722   del. 25/1/43
EE730   del. 22/2/43, cd Lizard, 23/3/43
BASES: Skeabrae, Perranporth, Lasham,
Fairlop

Spitfire IXb & IXe

October 1943-January 1944
March 1944-December 1944

During this period, the Squadron became
part of the newly formed 2nd ATAF, 83
Group, 125 Wing. 15/11/43 (prior to 'D' Day
6/6/44)

MH456   del. 6/10/43
MH479   del. 14/9/43
MH488   del. 7/9/43
MH492   del. 14/9/43
MH504   del. 26/9/43
MH508   del. 14/9/43
MH512   del. 6/10/43, LO-Q
MH526   del. 6/10/43, LO-D
MH708   del. 6/10/43
MH709   del. 6/10/43, LO-R, FTR ops
        16/6/44
MH713   LO-Y
MH716   del. 15/6/44
MH721   del. 6/10/43, FTR ops 21/12/44
MH722   del. 6/10/43, cd 7/1/44
MH724   del. 6/10/43
MH736   del. 15/6/44, LO-X
MH737
MH882   del. 28/10/44, LO-E
MJ132   LO-S
MJ147   LO-B
MJ171
MJ239
MJ276
MJ294   del. 5/10/44
MJ303   LO-O
MJ305   LO-K

MJ339   w/u fce/ldg Normandy Beach
        7/6/44. D L Kidd was the first to
        land in France!
MJ398   del. 15/6/44
MJ441   del. 28/9/44
MJ457   del. 28/9/44
MJ520
MJ528   del. 28/9/44
MJ605   del. 6/7/44
MJ848   del. 28/9/44
MJ873   del. 18/10/44
MJ881   LO-F
MJ884   del. 13/7/44
MK144   del. 28/7/44
MK200
MK230   del. 28/9/44
MK232   del. 15/6/44
MK244   del. 6/7/44
MK253
MK254
MK255   del. 15/6/44
MK366   del. 20/7/44
MK464   del. 28/9/44
MK611   LO-A
MK612   del. 15/6/44
MK614   del. 15/6/44
MK618   LO-S
MK624   del. 12/3/44
MK630
MK729   del. 28/9/44, cd/ld Coltishall
        14/10/44
MK755
MK775   del. 13/7/44. Flown by J J le Roux
        during the attack on what was
        later realised to be Rommel's
        staff-car, carrying the General
        himself.
MK793   del. 29/10/44
MK841   del. 13/7/44
MK882
MK999   del. 5/10/44
ML177   del. 13/7/44
ML205   del. 28/9/44
ML208   del. 26/10/44
ML244   del. 9/11/44
ML252   del. 15/6/44
ML264   del. 28/9/44
ML270   del. 19/10/44

ML307 del. 15/6/44
ML414 del. 28/9/44
NH150 del. 5/10/44
NH171
NH360
NH366 del. 10/8/44
NH380 del. 17/8/44
NH401 del. 27/10/44
NH470 del. 6/7/44, FTR ops 8/8/44
NH537 del. 17/8/44
NH549 del. 17/8/44
NH556 del. 10/8/44
NH591 del. 17/8/44
PL155 FTR ops 29/8/44
PL160 del. 17/8/44
PL191
PL207 del. 10/8/44
PL213 del. 10/8/44
PL264 del. 26/8/44
PL330 del. 24/8/44
PL344
PL430
PL436 del. 10/8/44
PL490 del. 10/8/44
PL493 del. 17/8/44
PL495 del. 14/9/44
PT396 del. 17/8/44
PT407

BASES: Newchurch, Detling, Ford, Longues (B11), Lingevres (B19), Nivillier (B40), Deurne (B70), Coltishall, Matlaske.

Spitfire L.F.Vb
January 1944-April 1944
W3375 del. 20/2/44
W3428 del. 1/3/44
W3624 del. 27/2/44
AA744 del. 26/2/44
AA979 del. 4/3/44
AB209 del. 25/1/44
AB898
AB916 del. 25/1/44
AD266 del. 25/1/44
AD374 del. 4/3/44
AD557
AR296
AR376 del. 25/1/44

BL304 del. 5/3/44
BL336 del. 6/3/44
BL418 del. 25/1/44
BL437 del. 25/1/44
BL525 del. 26/2/44
BL641 del. 4/3/44
BL686 del. 25/1/44
BL696 del. 25/1/44
BL718 del. 4/3/44
BL727 del. 25/1/44
BL787 del. 4/3/44
BL957 del. 25/1/44
BM200 del. 25/1/44
BM538 del. 4/3/44
BM583 del. 25/1/44
EN765 del. 4/4/44
EP767 del. 25/1/44
BASES: Skeabrae, Detling

Spitfire H.F.VII
January 1944-April 1944
MB763
MB828
MD114 DU-G (312 Sqn codes)
MD118
MD122
MD138
BASE: Skeabrae
N.B. These a/c were on the charge of Skeabrae Station Flight but flown by 602 Sqn.

Spitfire L.F.XVIe
27 November 1944-15 May 1945
SM234 del. 20/11/44
SM235 del. 20/11/44
SM254 del. 23/11/44
SM257 del. 27/11/44
SM276 del. 23/11/44
SM287 del. 27/11/44
SM288 del. 27/11/44
SM296 del. 23/11/44
SM301 del. 23/11/44
SM307 del. 25/11/44
SM341 del. 23/11/44
SM342 del. 22/12/44
SM343 del. 23/11/44, LO-H
SM350 del. 23/11/44

SM351 del. 23/11/44
SM352 del. 23/11/44
SM353 del. 23/11/44, coll with SM538, cd nr Swann 14/2/45
SM358 del. 22/12/44
SM361 del. 23/11/44
SM388 del. 23/11/44
SM400 del. 20/12/44
SM424 del. 23/11/44
SM538 del. 4/1/45, coll with SM353, cd nr Swann 14/2/45
TB382 del. 19/1/45, LO-Z   Now preserved with the RAF Exhibition Flight at Abingdon.
TB595 del. 26/3/45
TB911
TD123 del. 28/3/45
TD127 del. 27/3/45
BASES: Matlaske, Coltishall, Ludham and Coltishall where the Squadron disbanded on the 15 May 1945, thus ending its war-time 'embodiment' into the regular RAF.
COLOUR SCHEMES: No specific information is readily available for the war-time period but from existing photographs it can be seen that the Spitfires carried the standard fighter camouflage schemes and national insignia with varying styles of code lettering together with the Lion Rampant within a shield on the cowlings.

Auster I
March 1945-May 1945
LB349
BASES: Ludham, Coltishall

On the reformation of the Auxiliary Air Force in 1946, 602 Squadron reformed at their old base RNAS Abbotsinch, HMS Sanderling, on the 11th June 1946. History repeated itself with 602 again being the 'first' Auxiliary Squadron to do so.
Having flown only Spitfires throughout the war, 602 was again re-equipped with them (though not with 'Merlin'-engined aircraft, but with 'Griffon' variants).

Harvard T.2B
August 1946-October 1953

FT141	del. 31/7/47	RAI-Z(1)	Silver with yellow bands. w/o Abbotsinch 24/1/49, Pilot Archie Robinson DFC unhurt.
KF374	del. 13/8/46	RAI-Y/LO-Y	Tr cam/yellow/silver with yellow bands. First a/c delivered after post-war reformation.
KF389	del. 14/7/49	RAI-Z(2)/LO-X(2)	Silver with yellow bands.
KF442	del. 3/4/49		Yellow. WFU 2/9/49
KF584	del. 24/8/46	RAI-X/LO-X(1)	Yellow/silver with yellow bands.
KF920	del. 27/3/51	LO-Z	Silver with yellow bands.

BASES: Renfrew, Abbotsinch.

Spitfire F.14*FR.14E
October 1946-September 1948

MV253	del. 12/6/47	RAI-D?	SDF Cam.
RM753*	del. 4/3/47	RAI-C(1)?	SDF Cam. w/o Abbotsinch 22/6/47. SOC 11/8/47.
TP236	del. 24/10/46,	RAI-A	SDF Cam. First post-war Spitfire delivered Sqn
TX985	del. 1/12/46	RAI-B	
TX998	del. 29/7/47	RAI-C(2)	SDF Cam.

BASE: Abbotsinch

Spitfire F.21
April 1947-January 1951

LA193	del. 10/4/47	RAI-E	SDF Cam. w/o Woodvale, 10/6/48.
LA198	del. 12/5/47	RAI-G(1)	SDF Cam. Emergency ldg Horsham St Faith 22/7/49. Preserved as 'Gate Guardian' RAF Leuchars, June 1986.
LA211	del. 9/6/47	RAI-K(1)?	SDF Cam. w/o nr Fleetwood 23/7/47. Fg Off Ivor Reid killed.
LA222	del. 18/7/47	RAI-M	SDF Cam. w/o in fcc/ld nr Glenboig 31/10/48. P2 Jim Johnston DFC unhurt.
LA225	del. 6/6/47	RAI-J(1)	SDF Cam.
LA227	del. 10/3/49	RAI-O /LO-O	Silver
LA250	del. 10/4/47	RAI-F(1)	SDF Cam.
LA265	del. 14/9/48	RAI-J(3)	SDF Cam.
LA267	del. 8/2/49	RAI-M (2)/LO-M	Silver. (LO-M possibly in blue, Cooper Trophy 1950?)
LA268	del. 15/4/47	RAI-H(1)	SDF Cam. Spun-in and cd nr Bishopton, 3/4/48. Fg Off Hamish McWilliam killed.
LA269	del. 21/7/49	RAI-H(3)/LO-H	SDF Cam. ('D' roundels and fin flash)
LA275	del. 27/4/48	RAI-H(2)	SDF Cam. w/o Renfrew 18/6/49. Fg Off Jack Forrest unhurt.
LA279	del. 5/7/48	RAI-J(2)	SDF Cam. w/o Abbotsinch 26/7/48. Fg Off Archie Robinson DFC unhurt.
LA283	del. 17/2/49	RAI-N(1)?/LO-N(1)?	Silver?
LA315	del. 2/8/47	RAI-K(2)/LO-K	SDF Cam. (Silver spinner? July 1950)
LA319	del. 28/7/49	RAI-G(2)/LO-G	SDF Cam. ('D' roundels and fin flash)
LA329	del. 00/09/44	RAI-L(1)	SDF Cam. ('D' roundels and fin flash). w/o Renfrew 4/5/50

BASES: Abbotsinch, Renfrew

Spitfire F.22
September 1948-December 1951

PK321	del. 18/5/50	RAI-L(2)/LO-L	Silver
PK325	del. 3/9/50		SDF Cam.
PK349	del. 7/10/48	RAI-D/LO-D	SDF Cam.
PK369	del. 30/9/48	RAI-B/LO-B	SDF Cam.
PK395	del. 17/1/50	RAI-F/LO-F	SDF Cam.—very weathered (two-tone blue spinner 7/50, dark blue later)

PK407	del. 1/9/50		SDF Cam.
PK547	del. 3/6/50	LO-J	SDF Cam.
PK560	del. 7/10/48	RAI-C/LO-C	SDF Cam.
PK578	del. 30/9/48	RAI-A/LO-A	SDF Cam. (dark blue spinner)
PK606	del. 3/6/50	LO-P	
PK621	del. 15/1/50	RAI-E(2)/LO-E	SDF Cam.
PK630	del. 8/9/50		SDF Cam.
PK651	del. 3/6/50	LO-N(2)?	Silver (Blue spinner)

BASES: Abbotsinch, Renfrew

COLOUR SCHEMES Spitfires: SDF Cam = Standard post-war Day Fighter camouflage of dark green and ocean grey upper surfaces and medium sea grey under surfaces together with sky rear fuselage band and spinner, yellow outer wing leading edges and 'C/C1' roundels and fin flashes. Serials were in black on rear fuselage and under the wings.

Squadron 'RAI-' codes were in white but were perhaps sky when changed to 'LO-'. Some aircraft carried 'D' roundels and fin flash.

Silver = Post-war Fighter Command overall silver with 'D' roundels and fin flash, black serials and sodes, silver spinners were later changed to dark blue in 1950.

The last 'official' 602 Squadron Spitfire, PK651 LO-N, left from RAF Leuchars during the Squadron's mobilisation on 8th May 1951 some twelve years after the first Spitfire arrived on 8th May 1939. It was delivered to 102 FRS North Luffenham piloted by Flt Lt W B MacGregor. However three Spitfires were still under repair at Renfrew by 63MU, the last one PK321 LO-L, not departing until December 1951.

Vampire F.3
September 1952-November 1953

VF335	del. 27/9/52 'R' (not 602 Sqn code)	Silver
VT800	del. 27/9/52	Silver
VT812	del. 8/8/53	Silver. (carried two sets of roundels and serial numbers on booms during July 1953). Preserved RAF Museum.

BASE: Renfrew

Vampire FB.5
January 1951-March 1957

VV456	del. 16/1/51	LO-H	Silver
VV478	del. 4/5/56	'J'(2) (1/56)	SDF Cam. (Tartan markings).
VV567	del. 22/2/51	LO-K, 'K'	Silver/SDF Cam. (Codes then tartan markings, w/o, Abbotsinch 27/11/54. Pilot W W Galloway unhurt.
VX475	del. 9/2/51	LO-J, 'J'(1), 'H'(2) (7/56)	Silver/SDF Cam (Tartan Markings).
VZ105	del. 9/12/55	'G'(3)	SDF Cam. (Tartan markings)
VZ345	del. 12/1/54	LO-L(4), 'L'	SDF Cam. (Codes then tartan markings)
VZ812	del. 3/2/53	LO-C(2)	Silver
VZ831	del. 8/1/51	LO-B(1)	Silver. w/o nr Prestwick, 7/6/53. Pilot W M Agnew unhurt.
VZ841	del. 22/9/52	LO-L(3)	Silver
WA137	del. 16/1/51	LO-D, 'D'	Silver/SDF Cam. (Codes then tartan markings)
WA176	del. 14/1/55	'K'(2)	SDF Cam. (Tartan markings)
WA179	del. 15/1/51	LO-E, 'E'	Silver/SDF Cam. (Tartan markings)
WA182	del. 15/1/51	LO-C(1), 'B'	Silver/SDF Cam. (Tartan markings)
WA196	del. 18/1/51	LO-F, 'F'	Silver/SDF Cam. (Tartan markings)
WA216	del. 18/1/51	LO-G(1)	Silver

WA232	del. 8/1/51	LO-A(1)	Silver. w/o Inverbervie, 28/7/51. (Not being flown by 602 pilot).
WA315	del. 7/5/51	LO-L(1)	Silver
WA427	del. 28/6/51	LO-G(2), 'G'	Silver/SDF Cam. (Tartan markings)
WA453	del. 5/9/51	LO-A(2), 'A'	Silver/SDF Cam. (Tartan markings)
WE840	del. 26/4/52	LO-L(2)	Silver. Intentially landed wheels-up at Renfrew on 6/9/52 after mid-air collision over Greenock. Pilot Ian Hogg unhurt.

(WA398 'M' of 602 Sqn was used by 602 during July/August 1955).

BASES: Renfrew, Abbotsinch

Vampire FB.9
November 1954-February 1957

WR232	del. 25/6/56	'M'	MEAF Cam (Tartan markings). PR blue under surfaces.
WR261	del. 15/11/54	'C'	SDF Cam. (Tartan markings)

BASE: Abbotsinch

COLOUR SCHEMES: initially aircraft delivered in plain silver, 'LO' codes in black were soon applied to the booms together with the Squadron badge flanked by small tartan bars on the nose. In 1954 the aircraft were camouflaged in the Standard Day Flight scheme of dark green and dark sea grey upper surfaces with silver under surfaces. A few camouflaged aircraft retained the black 'LO' codes on the booms with only the Squadron badge transfer displayed on the nose. Eventually Grey Douglas tartan bars were applied to the booms each side of the roundel and the individual aircraft indentification letter was applied in black on the nose wheel door. In all schemes serials were black and roundels and fin flashes type 'D'.

The Vampire F.3s were only used temporarily and did not carry any 602 marks though VF335 bore an unknown squadron's badge on its nose along with its previous code 'R'. WR232 'M', one of the FB.9s, was finished in the Middle East scheme with blue undersurfaces but WR261 'C' was in the standard day fighter colours.

Meteor T.7
April 1951-February 1957

VW438	del. 16/4/51	LO-V(1)?	Silver. w/o nr Leuchars 23/6/51.
WA629	del. 20/4/54	'W'(2)	Silver. w/o Cromlix Estate 3/10/54.
WF773	del. 10/4/51	LO-W	Silver (red rims to engine nacelles from 1953).
WF816	allocated 4/5/51, no records exist of this a/c ever serving in the Sqn.		
WF846	del. 9/8/51	LO-V(2), 'V'	Silver (red rims to engine nacelles from 1953).
WG993	del. 27/4/56	'V'(3)	Silver
WL480	del. 25/10/54	'X'	Silver

BASES: Renfrew, Abbotsinch

COLOUR SCHEMES: Overall silver with yellow bands on rear fuselage and wings, black serial numbers on rear fuselage and under the wings 'D' roundels and fin flashes. 'LO' codes in black with individual identity letter repeated on the nose wheel door. Squadron badge flanked by small Grey Douglas tartan bars on outside of each engine nacelle on some aircraft. In 1954, WF846 at least, abandoned the 'LO' codes for large versions of the tartan markings each side of the fuselage roundel repeated on the wing tips. Intake rims reverted to silver and the Squadron badge with small tartan bars appeared below the windscreen.

Vampire T11
December 1956-February 1957
XD550   del. 3/12/56

BASE: Abbotsinch

COLOUR SCHEMES: Overall silver with yellow bands on booms and wings, black serials on booms and under wings, 'D' roundels and fin flashes. It is unlikely that any Squadron markings were applied.

NOTE: The Vampire FB.5 and Meteor T.7 aircraft allocated to the other two Scottish Auxiliaries Squadrons were delivered to Leuchars during the 1951 mobilisation. They were maintained by 602 who were already operating the types and some were flown by 602 pilots: e.g. Vampire WA398 (to 603 Sq), WA399 and WA401 (to 612 Sq) and Meteor WF 825 (to 603 Sq). 603 and 612 Squadrons both converted to Vampires while at Leuchars as neither of their home bases (Turnhouse and Dyce) were then suitable for jet aircraft operation. The Aberdeen Squadron took their aircraft to Edzell from where they operated while Dyce was being upgraded returning home on 2/11/52.

Dispersal of final complement of aircraft on disbandment, 1957.

Vampire FB.5/9
VX475   to 19MU, St Athan, 19/2/57.
VZ345   to 19MU, St Athan, 19/2/57.
WA137   to 19MU, St Athan, 19/2/57.
WA176   to 19MU, St Athan, 19/2/57.
WA196   to 19MU, St Athan, 19/2/57.
WA453   to 19MU, St Athan, 19/2/57.
WR261   to 19MU, St Athan, 20/2/57.
WA179   to 19MU, St Athan, 21/2/57.
VZ105   to 19MU, St Athan, 24/2/57.
VV478   to 19MU, St Athan, 24/3/57.

Vampire T.11
XD550   'Collected' by 1 Squadron and flown to Tangmere on 20/2/57.

Meteor T.7
WF846   to 12MU, Kirkbride, 19/2/57.
WG993   to 12MU, Kirkbride, 19/2/57.

602 Squadron aircraft still extant

Spitfire Ia
R6915

Delivered from 12MU on 21/1/41 to Prestwick, later flying from Ayr (Heathfield) it served until 6/7/41 when it passed to 61 OTU. Preserved and displayed at the Imperial War Museum, Lambeth.

Spitfire L.F.XVIe
TB382, LO-Z (7244M)

Delivered new from 6MU on 19/1/45 to Ludham where it was coded 'LO-Z'. Used for dive-bombing and recce missions it also flew from Coltishall. As a display air frame it was 'Gate Guardian' at RAF Middleton St George coded 'LO-X' for a time in the late 50s and early 60s and later was used in the film 'The Battle of Britain'. It is currently in use as a mobile exhibit with the RAF Exhibition Flight at Abingdon.

Spitfire L.F.XVIe
RW393 XT-A (7263M)

It would seem that this aircraft was actually allocated to 602 on 27/3/56 as an instructional airframe. However it arrived at RAF Turnhouse from 45MU (finished in white) and later became 'Gate Guardian' there with 603 codes as a memorial to the men of that Squadron.

Spitfire F21
LA198 RAI-G (7118M)

To 602 at Abbotsinch 12th May 1947. Damaged at Horsham St Faith 22/7/49 and did not return to 602. Preserved at RAF Locking until transfer to RAF Leuchars as 'Gate Guardian', June 1986, where it now rests in an impressive pose on a pylon and serves as a tangible memorial to the men of the City of Glasgow Squadron.

Vampire F 3
VT812 (7200M)

Flew with 602 Squadron from 8th August 1952 until 23rd November 1953. Came from North Weald and went to 48MU. During annual camp at RAF Tangmere in 1953 it sported two sets of roundels and serial numbers on its booms! Now preserved in the RAF Museum, Hendon, bearing the markings of 601 Squadron.

Spitfire L.F.XVIe TB308 ('LO-D' after its use at Bishopbriggs) (7255M)

To 602 Squadron on 12th August 1955, from 45MU Kinloss for instructional purposes, then as a 'Gate Guardian' for the new terminal at Glasgow's civil terminal at Renfrew. It was prepared, camouflaged in a spurious scheme of brown and green with blue under surfaces and type 'D' roundels and fin flash. It was intended to mount the aircraft on a plinth, however, such were the official requirements, that the idea had to be abandoned. When 602 was disbanded, the aircraft went to RAF Bishopbriggs (near Glasgow) as their 'Gate Guardian', having been displayed at least once, during 'Battle of Britain' Week in Paisley. The engine had been partially dismantled to reduce weight for mounting. With the closure of Bishopbriggs the aircraft went to RAF Norton (near Sheffield) on 6/3/58, then the RAF Hospital at Ely, eventually being scrapped at RAF Bicester.

Tailpiece

Post-war flying hours (day and night) by 602 Squadron, 1946-1957 (as accurate as available information allows)

Year	Aircraft	Hours
1946	Harvard, Spitfire F14	27.25
1947	Harvard, Spitfire F14, F21	900.51
1948	Harvard, Spitfire F14, F21, F22	(661. no records for April, May, June, July or August).
1949	Harvard, Spitfire F21, F22	1100 approx
1950	Harvard, Spitfire F21, F22	1384.25
1951	Harvard, Spitfire F22, Vampire FB5, Meteor T7. (+2.35 on a Balliol!)	1296.10
1952	Harvard, Vampire F3, FB5, Meteor T7	1312.30
1953	Harvard, Vampire F3, FB5, Meteor T7	1000 (approx)
1954	Vampire FB5, Meteor T7	2313.20
1955	Vampire FB5, FB9, Meteor T7	2568.25
1956	Vampire FB5, FB9, Meteor T7 (+1.35 on Vampire T11 and 7.25 on Meteor F8)	2487.30
1957	Vampire FB5, FB9, Meteor T7	35.25
	Total hours (approx)	15,000
	Total Spitfire hours	2032.30 (approx)
	Total Harvard hours	1487.42 (approx)
	Total Vampire hours	8507.10 (approx)
	Total Meteor hours	1648.35 (approx)

Back from his first flight in a jet
aircraft comes the 17-year-old Marquess
of Clydesdale (left), son of the Duke of
Hamilton (right), Honorary Air
Commodore of 602 Squadron. During
the flight in the Meteor the Marquess, a
pilot of the Eton College Air Cadet
Force, took over the controls from the
Squadron's CO, Squadron Leader R. B.
Davidson, DFC (centre).
The Marquess who inherited the title
in 1972, became a pilot in the RAF
qualifying as a flying instructor,
instrument rating examiner and
subsequently, a test pilot with Scottish
Aviation.

Aircraft Markings

Badges

Initially 602 Squadron was a light bomber unit and prior to the general introduction of the standard format RAF badge in the mid/late 1930's 602 had a design based upon the City of Glasgow's own Coat of Arms. (Tree, Bird, Fish, Bell, surmounted by RAF Wings). This badge appeared on some aircraft i.e. Wapitis and Harts.

In June 1937, H.M. King George VI approved the official badge as prepared by the Chester Herald, then as now, the 'Inspector of RAF Badges'. This was the familiar saltire outline on which there was superimposed a Lion Rampant within the now standard format for RAF Badges. Also approved was the motto:

'CAVE LEONEM CRUCIATUM'
(Beware the crossed lion)

This badge, or a version within a 'grenade' outline (as for Bomber Squadrons) was used on some aircraft pre-war such as the Hind.

The full badge, on Vampires and Meteors, was initially combined with small tartan flashes (see later) on the noses of the Vampires and engine nacelles or noses of Meteor 7's. The badges being initially hand painted, were later applied by transfer.

Identification Letters

The Gauntlets bore 'LO' code letters plus an individual aircraft letter then, with the introduction of the Spitfire in May 1939, the code letters 'ZT' were used being painted on fuselage sides in a medium sea grey.

On, or just before the outbreak of war, all RAF Squadron codes were changed 602's reverting to 'LO'. These were used throughout the war being applied in 'medium sea grey' and 'sky' as the camouflage colours changed.

After the war, on reforming as an Auxiliary unit within Reserve Command, the code letters 'RAI' were issued (the Auxiliary Squadrons being in the RAA to RAW sequence). After the transfer back to Fighter Command in November 1949 the Auxiliaries began to revert to their wartime codes. This was apparently quite a slow process and it would seem that 602's aircraft were not recoded 'LO' until the second half of 1950 (at least some aircraft were still in 'RAI' marks at the annual camp, RAF Chivenor in July 1950, i.e. Spitfire F22, PK395, RAI-F).

During 1954 however, with the general application of camouflage, the code letters ceased to be used and large 'Grey Douglas' tartan markings were applied each side of the roundel, together with the existing individual aircraft letter on the nosewheel door in black.

Both the 'RAI' and 'LO' codes were applied in white, or perhaps 'sky', on the camouflaged Spitfires and black on the silver aircraft. Some variation in the style of lettering is noticeable.

The Vampire and Meteor aircraft, initially silver finished, had black codes and this was continued on a few of the Vampires when they were camouflaged in 1954.

The Harvards were delivered in a variety of schemes. One had green/brown camouflage with yellow undersides; they were re-finished all over yellow and had black 'RAI' codes. Those that were silver and those yellow ones refinished silver, had black 'LO' codes applied during 1951. It should be noted that even as late as the Press Day for the introduction of the Vampire, (Saturday 27th January 1951), the Harvards still bore 'RAI' codes. They were changed soon after.

Markings

Pre-war, the markings on the D.H.9As and Fawns are not known, indeed they may not have had any (as witness such photos as are available), though some of the Fawns and 504s had thin coloured bands either side of the roundel along the fuselage. Avro 504s were marked '602' in black (some evidence suggests that they might have had the '602' in Flight colours, however). The Wapitis, Harts and Hinds also had the '602' applied. The three flights—'A', 'B' and 'C'—marked their aircraft in red, yellow and blue respectively. The Gauntlets were camouflaged, being referred to by letter in the programme for the Empire Air Day, 20th May 1939.

During the war, the Spitfires had a variety of individual emblems applied to them by their pilots, including nick-names, and the names representing the presenters of particular aircraft. Whilst at Drem (1939/40) 'B' flight aircraft bore the names of Snow White's dwarfs (e.g. Sandy Johnstone's aircraft was 'Bashful' and George Pinkerton's 'Grumpy')! When at Kenley, the Spitfires bore on their cowlings a shield containing the lion rampant, 'A' Flight aircraft having a white shield and 'B' Flight an orange one, a practice continued on the Spitfire IXs and on the XVIs as well.

Post-war, neither the Spitfires nor Harvards bore actual Squadron markings (as opposed to code letters) though those Spitfire F.22s which came from other Auxiliary Squadrons during 1950 might well have maintained their coloured spinners (e.g. red and yellow spinners from 608 Sqn). During 1950, however, the camouflaged Spitfires had dark spinners probably standard black (or possibly dark blue). With the advent of the Vampire during January 1951, these aircraft soon had the Squadron badge with small Grey Douglas tartan flashes on each side of the nose, plus black 'LO' code letters and individual letters on the booms. The Harvards bore no markings other than code and individual letters in black.

Officially, like the regular RAF Squadrons, code letters should have been abandoned by the late forties or early fifties and replaced by coloured squadron markings. An official scheme had been prepared which included the Auxiliaries though 602 did not seem to accept what may have been proposed for them—the nature of which is still the subject of debate. Some sources have suggested a blue/green pattern but the pattern actually applied was a version of their official tartan—the Grey Douglas. As applied to the Vampires, it was similar to that on the Squadron board—the colours being black, grey and white.

On the Meteor T7s a similar arrangement was initially applied on the front of the engine nacelles in addition to 'LO' coding. Individual letters for Vampire and Meteor aircraft were repeated on the nosewheel door in black.

During 1951, 603 (City of Edinburgh) Squadron began to apply their official markings to their Spitfires—two horizontal black or very dark blue bars between which there was a *light blue* and *red* check pattern. These markings were later carried on their Vampires and Meteors.

612 (County of Aberdeen) Squadron followed the Glasgow Squadron pattern with their Squadron badge flashed by small tartan flashes on each side of the nose of their Vampires, together with black code letters. Their tartan was, unsurprisingly, the 'Hunting Gordon'. In both cases, the tartan applied had to be a simplified version of the real thing.

St. James's Palace, S.W.

17th June, 1933.

My Dear Ellington,

I write with further reference to your letter
of the 20th June concerning the proposal to introduce a
kilted uniform for the Pipe Bands of the two Scottish
Squadrons of the Auxiliary Air Force.

The Prince of Wales spoke to the King on the
subject, with the result that I sent your letter and the
sketch to Sir Clive Wigram, who now replies as follows:-

"I have submitted to the King your letter and that
from the Chief of the Air Staff together with the sketch
of the proposed uniform for the Pipe Bands of the two
Scottish Squadrons of the Auxiliary Air Force, of which
His Majesty approves."

I return herewith the sketch which you sent.

Yours very sincerely,

Lionel Halsey.

Air Chief Marshal Sir Edward L. Ellington,
            K.C.B.,C.M.G., C.B.E.,
Air Ministry,
KINGSWAY.

Squadron Bases

Base	From	Aircraft
Renfrew	15th September 1925	DH9A
		Avro 504K
		Avro 504N
		Fawn I, II & III
		Wapiti I, II & VI
Abbotsinch	20th January 1933	Wapiti II & VI
		Avro 504N
		Hart I & Trainer
		Tutor
		Hind & Hind Trainer
		Hector
		Gauntlet II
		Battle
		Spitfire I/Ia
		Harvard I
		Magister
Grangemouth	7th October 1939, (temporarily)	Magister
		Harvard I
		Battle II
		Spitfire Ia
Drem	13th October 1939	Spitfire Ia
		Tiger Moth II
Dyce ('B' Flt)	14th April 1940	Spitfire Ia
Montrose ('A' Flt)		
Drem	28th May 1940	Spitfire Ia
		DH82A
Westhampnett	13th August 1940	Spitfire Ia
Prestwick	17th December 1940	Spitfire Ia
Ayr (Heathfield)	15th April 1941 (opening date)	Spitfire Ia
		Spitfire IIa
Kenley	10th July 1941	Spitfire IIa
	30th July 1941	Spitfire Vb
Redhill	14th January 1942	Spitfire Vb
		Spitfire Vc
Kenley	4th March 1942	Spitfire Vb
		Spitfire Vc
Redhill	13th May 1942	Spitfire Vb
		Spitfire Vc

Base	From	Aircraft
Peterhead	17th July 1942	Spitfire Va, Vb
Skeabrae ('A' Flt)	10th September 1942	Spitfire Va, Vb, Vc
Sumburgh ('B' Flt)		Spitfire H.F.VI
Perranporth	20th January 1943	Spitfire Vb, Vc
Lasham	14th April 1943	Spitfire Vb, Vc
Fairlop	29th April 1943	Spitfire Vb, Vc
Bognor	1st June 1943	Spitfire Vb
Kingsnorth	1st July 1943	Spitfire Vb
Newchurch	13th August 1943	Spitfire Vb
Detling	12 October 1943	Spitfire Vb
		Spitfire IXb
Skeabrae	18th January 1944	Spitfire L.F.Vb
		Spitfire VII
Detling	12th March 1944	Spitfire IXb
Llanbedr	13th March 1944	Spitfire IXb
Detling	20th March 1944	Spitfire IXb
Ford	18th April 1944	Spitfire IXb
B11 Longues	25th? June 1944	Spitfire IXe
B19 Lingevres	13th August 1944	Spitfire IXe
B40 Nivilliers	2nd September 1944	Spitfire IXe
B70 Deurne	17th September 1944	Spitfire IXe
Coltishall	29th September 1944	Spitfire IXb
Matlaske	18th October 1944	Spitfire IXb
	27th November 1944	Spitfire L.F.XVIe
Ludham	23rd February 1945	Spitfire L.F.XVIe
		Auster I
Coltishall	5th April 1945	Spitfire L.F.XVIe
		Auster I

Disbanded at **Coltishall** 15th May 1945.   Reformed at **RNAS Abbotsinch** on 11th June 1946, as a Fighter Squadron of the Auxiliary Air Force.

Base	From	Aircraft
Abbotsinch	11th June 1946	Spitfire F.14/FR.14E
		Spitfire F.21
		Spitfire F.22
		Harvard T.2B
Renfrew	June 1949	Spitfire F.21
		Spitfire F.22
		Harvard T.2B
	from 8/1/51	Vampire FB.5
		Vampire F.3
		Meteor T.7
Abbotsinch	18th June 1954	Vampire FB.5
		Vampire FB.9
		Vampire T.11
		Meteor T.7

Disbanded at RNAS Abbotsinch on 10th March 1957 in compliance with the decision to disband all the flying squadrons of the Royal Auxiliary Air Force.

In addition to their operational airfield bases each Auxiliary squadron enjoyed a town headquarters for training and for the rich social life which characterised the Auxiliaries, at least before the war. The Glasgow squadron were, in 1925, initially accommodated in a wooden hut within 52 (Lowland Division) Signals drill hall at Jardine Street. In 1927 a new Town HQ was built by the local Territorial Association at 49 Coplaw Street and inspected by King George V on 12th of July 1927. The HQ was still in use by 602 on disbanding in March 1957. Nearby to Abbotsinch, Abbotsburn House was sold to the Air Ministry by a former CO of 602 Squadron, John Fullerton, and used by the Squadron for social and domestic purposes though it took some time after the War for it to be made ready once again. It was demolished some time after disbandment.

*Bill MacGregor in the cockpit of
a newly delivered Vampire jet at
Renfrew on the occasion of the press
visit to 602, 27th January 1951. H M
Stephen the C.O. expresses his
confidence along with Messrs. Bowman,
Daly, McGuire, Laird, Paxton, Robinson,
Reid, Johnston, Maxwell and Askins.*

Annual Summer Camps

Usually held during the last two weeks of July in the 'Glasgow Fair' trades holiday.

		Operational Aircraft
1926	RAF Leuchars	DH9A
1927	RAF Leuchars	DH9A
1928	RAF Leuchars	Fawn
1929	RAF Leuchars	Fawn
1930	RAF Leuchars	Wapiti
1931	RAF Hawkinge	Wapiti
1932	RAF Hawkinge	Wapiti
1933	RAF Hawkinge	Wapiti
1934	RAF Lympne	Hart
1935	RAF North Coates Fittes (First Auxiliary Squadron to carry out an armament practice camp)	Hart
1936	RAF Tangmere	Hind
1937	Rochford (Southend)	Hind
1938	RAF Hawkinge	Hind
1939	RAF Church Fenton	Spitfire I

After reformation 1946:

1947	RAF Woodvale	Spitfire FR.14 and F.21
1948	RAF Tangmere	Spitfire FR.14 and F.21
1949	RAF Horsham St Faith	Spitfire F.21 and F.22
1950	RAF Chivenor	Spitfire F.21 and F.22
1951	3 months mobilisation 15th April until 13th July 1951 at RAF Leuchars, including armament practice camp at RAF Acklington.	Vampire FB.5
1952	RAF Celle, Germany	Vampire FB.5
1953	RAF Tangmere	Vampire FB.5
1954	RAF Pembrey	Vampire FB.5
1955	RAF Horsham St Faith	Vampire FB.5 and FB.9
1956	RAF North Front, Gibraltar	Vampire FB.5 and FB.9

Maintenance Units (MUs) used by 602 Squadron aircraft
1946-1957

6MU	RAF Brize Norton	Spitfire
9MU	RAF Cosford	Spitfire
10MU	RAF Hullavington	Vampire F.3
12MU	RAF Kirkbride	Meteor T.7
19MU	RAF St Athan	Vampire FB.5 and FB.9
29MU	RAF High Ercall	Spitfire
33MU	RAF Lyneham	Spitfire
45MU	RAF Kinloss	Spitfire instructional airframes
48MU	RAF Hawarden	Vampire F.3
58MU	RAF Newton	Spitfire

63MU RAF Carluke, RAF Montrose then RAF Edzell. Repairs, etc. working parties to Abbotsinch and Renfrew—Spitfires and Vampires.

Plus Repair & Salvage Unit at RAF Honiley for Spitfires and 43 Group for Harvards.

ACKNOWLEDGEMENTS

I would like to thank the following for their help, enthusiasm and where appropriate for the use of their photographs.

Ex-Members of 602 (City of Glasgow) Squadron.

His Grace, The Duke of Hamilton and
  Brandon
D C Bartman (CO 1956/57)
Ian Blair DFM
R C Bridges
R G Burnett
J V P Daly
R B Davidson DFC (CO 1953/56)
J A Forrest (CO 1952/53)
W W Galloway
A M Grant AE
H J Henderson
E A Howell OBE DFC
A Jeffrey AE
D M Jack AE
A V R Johnstone CB DFC AE
(CO 1940/41)
J A Johnston DFC
J Kiddle
J E Lake AE
Mrs A D McNab (widow of Flt Lt A D McNab)

W F Larkin
D L Lloyd
W B MacGregor
W M McKinnon
C H MacLean AE
Glen Niven
J Parker
G C Pinkerton OBE DFC AE
(CO 1940)
A Richardson
Marcus Robinson CB AFC AE
(CO 1956/57)
A W Robinson DFC
S J Robinson
J Russell
A Taylor
J D Urie AE
A Young
T L Wright
P C Webb CBE DFC AE

Together with aviation enthusiasts:

G Cruickshank
R Lindsay
T MacFadyen
A MacGregor
R Montgomery
R Pauline
J D R Rawlings

I G Stott
R C Sturtivant. (What could one
do without Ray!)
W G White (Without whose
photographs the Post-War visual
record would be minimal.)

Also Douglas McRoberts. Whose book 'Lions Rampant' is a splendid account of the story of 602 Squadron, and most certainly, the staff of the Air Historical Branch MOD. The Inspectorate of Recruiting, RAF. The Royal Air Force Museum Hendon, the Imperial War Museum, Lambeth and the Public Records Office at Kew.

Bibliography
'Fighter Squadrons of the RAF'—J D R Rawlings, MacDonalds
'Enemy in the Sky'—Air Vice Marshal AVR. Sandy Johnstone. William Kimber
'Spitfire—The History'—Eric B Morgan and Edward Shacklady, Key Publishing
'Where No Angels Dwell'—Air Vice Marshal AVR. Sandy Johnstone.
William Kimber
'Adventure In The Sky'—Air Vice Marshal AVR. Sandy Johnstone. William Kimber
Plus Various 'Air Britain' Publications.

The Operations Record Book (Form 540) 602 Squadron (1925-1957)

Back issues of the *'Glasgow Herald'* and the *'The Bulletin'* have also proved most useful, together with the help and assistance of the staff of the *'Glasgow Herald'* and their photographic library along with the Quadrant Picture Library *('Flight')*.

It has been difficult to trace the ownership of some photographs and apologies are offered to anyone whose help in this respect is not acknowledged.

I am particularly grateful to my colleagues at the Glasgow School of Art, James Murray who designed the book and Fraser Ross who did the typesetting.

To Alan Carlaw, my partner in Squadron Prints goes my gratitude for his patience, invaluable assistance and support in the massive job of editing the material.

Also, Bill McConnell of the 602 Museum Association for making available all records etc held in the Museum.

Epilogue
(From the programme of the Cooper Trophy presentation, June 1956)

The Auxiliaries gather at Abbotsinch every week-end when the following may be encountered:—

A sleek Vampire taxis to the dispersal, an aircraft marshaller signalling to the pilot guides the aircraft expertly to its position on the line, as it pivots swiftly its engine gives a final scream before lapsing into silence and immobility. Before the exhaust fumes have diffused into the atmosphere, a fuel bowser trundles towards the stationary aircraft, and in an instant the refuelling team is replenishing the supplies of the aircraft tanks.

The Pilot by now has extracted himself from his harness and is proceeding to the Flight Office where he will sign the after flight certificate and report to the N.C.O. any aircraft defects he has encountered.

When refuelling has been completed the ground crew will make particular checks on the aircraft. If defects have been reported they will be rectified by the section concerned. The certificate of serviceability will be signed by the respective responsible airmen, and the aircraft will be ready for the next sortie.

This procedure is common to fighter squadrons, but there is one major difference, the men taking part are "Auxiliaries." For five days these men are Civil Servants, Chemists, Teachers, Salesmen, Craftsmen, Clerks, Technicians, Draughtsmen and Tradesmen. For the other two days they are Pilots, Engine Fitters, Airframe Mechanics, Electricians, Cooks and Armourers. They are an asset to the squadron and an integral part of Great Britain's defence.

At present the squadron is almost up to full strength, but there are a limited number of vacancies for those of experience who apply for entry as trained Auxiliaries, or for those with the ability and initiative to learn a trade during their service with the Squadron.

Men joining the squadron prior to their National Service training have an excellent opportunity of doing their National Service with the squadron, providing they reach a satisfactory standard while serving as Auxiliaries.

```
To:-        Air Officer Commanding,
            No.2 Bomber Group,
            Royal Air Force,
            Andover.

From:-      Officer Commanding,
            No.602 (B) Squadron,
            Auxiliary Air Force,
            Abbotsinch.

Date:-      28th June, 1937.

    Subject:-  HIGHLAND MESS KIT.
```

Sir,

      I have the honour to request approval of the following details of Kilt Mess Kit for Officers of No.602 Squadron.

      On 31st July, 1936, we received a letter from Air Ministry, ref: 400273/35/S.7(c), approving the wearing of grey Douglas tartan kilt mess kit by Auxiliary Officers of Scottish Auxiliary Squadrons, and we have now worked out the details of the new mess dress described below and shown on the accompanying photographs, for your approval.

Head-dress	- New Field Service Cap.
Greatcoat	- Normal R.A.F. pattern.
Jacket & Waistcoats	- do.
Kilt	- Grey Douglas Tartan worsted kilt - military pleating. Height from floor, when kneeling, 1½".
Sporran	- White goathair Sporran mounted on gilt top, with Squadron Crest in centre of top and one albatross in each corner. Five short black tassels mounted on gilt bells with Squadron Crest.
Hose	- R.A.F. blue and white diced hose.
Garter Flashes	- Gold art silk braid 1¾" wide, 5¾" in length, with four ¾" pleats mounted on black elastic.
Skean Dhu	- Hand carved ebony handle with cairngorm stone in chased gilt mount. Steel blade. Black morocco leather sheath with chased gilt mountings.
Shoes	- Latchet brogue black patent leather shoes.
Laces	- Gold cord laces with gold tassels.

      I have the honour to be, Sir,

      Your obedient Servant,

Duncan Dyce. S/L.

CITY OF SQUADRON 602 GLASGOW BOMBER